With Tears
in
My Heart

Poetic
Meditations
of a Christian Woman

by
Gertrude Grace Sanborn
(1904-1988)

With Tears in My Heart—the Poems of Gertrude Grace Sanborn

Published by

THE BIBLE FOR TODAY PRESS
900 Park Avenue
Collingswood, New Jersey 08108
U.S.A.

Phone: 856-854-4452
Orders: 1-800-John 10:9
E-mail: BFT@BibleForToday.org
Website: www.BibleForToday.org
Fax: 856-854-2464

May 2005
B.F.T. #3196

Copyright 2005
All Rights Reserved
ISBN 1-56848-046-6

TABLE OF CONTENTS

Folio I---------Tears 9
Folio II--------The Bible..23
Folio III-------The Incarnation 41
Folio IV-------The Saviour 49
Folio V--------The Shepherd 65
Folio VI-------Calvary..73
Folio VII------Christ's Session..................................83
Folio VIII-----Christ's Second Coming....................89
Folio IX-------Christian Service 99
Folio X--------God's Will..121
Folio XI-------Death...135
Folio XII------Heaven 149
Folio XIII-----The Holy Spirit.................................159
Folio XIV-----Prayer..165
Folio XV------Nature..207
Folio XVI-----Audrey June 235
Folio XVII----Beverly Grace 251
Folio XVIII---Children 265
Folio XIX-----My Husband......................................279
Folio XX------Yvonne...287
Folio XXI-----My Mother 301
Folio XXII----Father 307
Folio XXIII---Other Family Members 313
Folio XXIV---Christian Love 323
Folio XXV----Bitterness 381
Folio XXVI---Grief...393
Folio XXVII--Christ's First Coming......................407

FOREWORD

How do I begin to tell you what my mother's poems have meant to me? How do I tell you of their comfort to my soul? They are the very essence of her personality. They have sprung from the fountain of her being--her inner-self, her private thought-sanctuary. She wrote through her tears of disappointments and griefs. She wrote of her victories over self and despair. She wrote of her joys and spiritual blessings.

She wrote about her life and all that made up that life--her longings, her disappointments, and her deep desires. She spoke of her family--her parents, her children, her husband, and even his family. Friends enjoyed her words. At birthdays or special occasions, she would bring a poem as a treasured gift. After a sermon, she would pen her gleanings. In despair, her pen met the page. In happiness, her days were recorded. As we read her writings, we feel her needs and witness her answered prayers.

Most of all, Gertrude Sanborn revealed her love of the Lord Jesus Christ and her devotion to the Scripture. The years of caring for her youngest daughter Beverly had kept her home "by the stuff" (I Samuel 30:24), forcing her to retreat into the promises of God. While other women would be a part of the community's social life, Mother would be home with her retarded daughter caring for Beverly's needs. When her household tasks would be

Foreword

completed, it was not unusual to find Mother in deep study of her precious King James Bible. It was from that Bible that she found strength to go on.

You may ask why I have chosen to title this book *With Tears in My Heart*. I do so because I know of the tears she had shed. Yet I saw in her life, a woman yielding to the will of God, come what may. I saw her victory in spite of the tears. She and my father Ren Sanborn were stalwarts of the faith, the kind you and I read about in the pages of the Bible.

May you, too, be blessed by the meditations of my mother's heart. May they be acceptable in God's sight. And may you also accept them as yours and be spiritually refreshed by her words (Psalm 19:14). This is my prayer for you.

In God's care,

Yvonne S. Waite

Yvonne Sanborn Waite
(the author's firstborn)

ACKNOWLEDGMENTS

To our Heavenly Father for His goodness and kindness in permitting the book to be published.

To Gertrude Sanborn (1904-1988) for writing such beautiful poetry for us to pass on to future generations.

To her granddaughter Audrey Dianne Cosby for her labor of love in typing all of the poems into computer-form many years ago, and for her encouragement to publish the poems in memory of her grandmother.

To her grandson Donald A. Waite, Jr., for the major task of finalizing the poems for printing. This included inserting Scripture verses and pictures, re-working the punctuation, and finalizing page-layout and font selection.

To her grandson Daniel S. Waite for his book publishing expertise and advice--without which we could not publish.

To her grandson David W. Waite for his love of his grandmother and her poetry.

To her grandson Richard N. Waite who remembers his Grandmother's spiritual insight and love for the Word of God.

To her son-in-law Dr. D. A. Waite for his encouragement in this project and for the difficult job of originally organizing the poems for publication.

Acknowledgments and Dedication

To Tamara A. Waite (Dan's wife) for her cover layout and design suggestions.

To Megan Y. Cosby (Dianne's daughter) and to Jeanette A. Waite (Don's wife) for their artistic and layout advice.

To Gertrude's husband R. O. Sanborn (1903-1988) for funds for such a publication.

To all of you who will get this book and be enriched by it, God bless!

DEDICATION

This book is dedicated to all those who have spiritual hunger for a closer walk with the Lord Jesus Christ.

May you see Him afresh and love Him anew as you read Gertrude Sanborn's poetry.

It is our desire that these poems be quoted and used to illustrate Biblical truths. The publisher, therefore, gives permission to quote up to five poems in a single sermon or publication—as long as the author and publisher are mentioned.

Folio I

Tears

And God shall wipe away
all tears from their eyes;
and there shall be no more death,
neither sorrow, nor crying,
neither shall there be any more pain:
for the former things are passed away.
Revelation 21:4

With Tears in My Heart

With dry eyes, Lord,
I stand before the world
And this is as it must be;
Yet in my heart there are tears.

Tears for my weakness in body
Tears for rebellion and loss
Tears for others who need Thee
Tears for the price of the Cross.

Tears in my heart, blessed weeping,
Or cold I would be and unmoved.
Lord, keep me weeping
With tears in my heart
Lest, prayerless,
I become disapproved.

July 1960

**For thou hast delivered my soul from death,
mine eyes from tears,
and my feet from falling.**
Psalm 116:8

Folio I—Tears

My Tears

All of my tears and my weepings
Because of my trials below
I placed at the feet of my Saviour
And under His smile they glow.

There, the tear-drops seemed jewels
Of rare and costly acclaim;
I shed them because of my children
I offered the Lord in His name.

1951

**Put thou my tears into thy bottle:
are they not in thy book?**
Psalm 56:8

Cry in the Morning

Cry all your tears in the morning
Go forth with a smile to the day
Weep out your burden to Jesus
Knowing he will sustain all the way.

Cry all your doubts and your heartaches
Tell Him your griefs and your fear
Cry all your tears in the morning
Then go forth thru the day with His cheer.

Mercies anew every morning
Exchanging His peace for your need
Bring all your tears to the Saviour
For none other will truly heed.

1970

Cast thy burden upon the LORD,
and he shall sustain thee:
he shall never suffer
the righteous to be moved.
Psalm 55:22

Folio I--Tears

Tears for the Nation

Tears for the lost and the dying
Tears for they've never been told
Tears for the youth who have wandered
Tears for the sick and the old.

Tears for our land and its freedoms
Tears for the flag that I love
Tears for the plight of our nation
Turned from our great God above.

Tears for my weakness of body
Tears for rebellion and love
Tears for others who serve Thee
Tears for the price of His cross.

Tears in my heart, blessed weepings,
Or cold I would be and unmoved
Lord, keep me serving with tears in my heart
Lest, prayerless, I become disapproved.

1968

📖

A time to weep, and a time to laugh
Ecclesiastes 3:4a

Tears for Others

I saw you crying
And saw reserve fall before the tears.
I heard you crying,
And heard you mourn
For those who have no fears.

I saw you crying
And felt the wall of strangeness melt away.
I saw you crying
And I knew you better
Than I did the other day.

I saw you crying
And rejoiced it was a Godly sorrow;
I felt your grief
That some should perish
Before today becomes tomorrow.

I saw you crying;
I cried, too, to see you weep;
I saw your sadness, and I began to pray
That someone else
Would yearn for others
In that way.

Folio I--Tears

O for more tears for those in darkness;
O for more lips to sing His praise;
O for more hearts to yearn for others;
O for more feet to walk His ways.

1938
This was written in LaGrange, Ohio when the author saw her friend, Clara Cruver, weeping because her father was unsaved and bound for Hell.

**I have great heaviness
and continual sorrow
in my heart . . . for
my brethren, my kinsmen
according to the flesh:**
Romans 9:2-3

No Time For Tears

No time for tears for I would serve Him;
No time for tears for night draws nigh;
No tears today for souls are dying;
No time for weeping, no time to cry.

No time for tears tho I have sorrow;
No times for tears tho I have loss;
No time to mourn for I have Jesus;
And He will help me bear my cross.

No time for tears for He's my comfort;
No time for tears since He's my friend;
No tears today to waste my hours,
For I must haste His word to send.

No time for tears since He's my Refuge;
No time for tears to dim my eyes;
No tears today--it's time for working;
Not time to grieve or wonder why.

No time for tears--it's time for singing;
No time for tears--it's time to praise;
No time to spend in lonely sighing;
No time for tears, no time to cry.

Tears

God gives us tears
To wash away the heartache,
To bathe our grief,
And dim our present loss.

God gives us tears--
They are a heavenly comfort.
They give release
And help us bear our cross.

God gives us tears--
We could not bear without them
The lonely hours
To learn to live again.

He gives us tears
But promises to dry them
And tell us why
We suffered grief and pain.

Let tears run down like a river day and night: give thyself no rest; let not the apple of thine eye cease.
Lamentations 2:18b

Blessed Lonely Desolations

Blessed lonely desolations,
Blessed hour I found no friend,
Blessed day when tears kept falling,
Blessed night that had no end.

For 'tis then I found my Refuge
As I fled to Jesus' feet;
There He held in sweet compassion,
There He all my grief did meet.

Had I never been so lonely
Had I never needed grace,
I would ne'er have looked to Jesus,
Really seen His tender face.

So I thank Him for the journey
Thru the valley and the test,
For I needed just that lesson
So I'd learn He knoweth best.

1946

**For God hath caused me to be fruitful
in the land of my affliction.**
Genesis 41:52b

Folio I--Tears

With Every Day

With every day, I find a greater solace
To come to Thee in confidence and faith;
For at Thy feet I find the peace to live by
And rest my case upon the Word Thou saith.

Then all my tears of sorrow, in repentance,
Become released before Thy Throne of Grace;
And there are changed to precious jewels of comfort
When faith removes the Veil before my face.

Then it is I find the Great Jehovah
To be the loving Jesus, Lord, and King;
And all my cares I lay before His scepter,
And from His throne new confidences bring.

July 1960 (Later put to music)

But we all, with open face
beholding as in a glass
the glory of the Lord,
are changed
into the same image
from glory to glory,
even as by
the Spirit of the Lord.
2 Corinthians 3:18

With Tears in My Heart—the Poems of Gertrude Grace Sanborn

Sorrowing Yet Rejoicing

Strangely sweet
It is to me
And wonderfully clear
That, though my heart is saddened
And there's in mine eye a tear,
He gives me light
And peace and joy
And causes me to sing.
His precious Word
Has strengthened me
And caused the bells to ring!

April 1953

As sorrowful, yet alway rejoicing;
as poor, yet making many rich;
as having nothing, and yet possessing all things.
2 Corinthians 6:10

Gertrude & Ren Sanborn on November 16, 1973
(Their Fiftieth Wedding Anniversary)

🔔

📖

𝔚hom have 𝔍 in heaven *but thee?*
and *there is* none upon earth *that* 𝔍 desire beside thee.
𝔐y flesh and my heart faileth:
but 𝔊od *is* the strength of my heart,
and my portion for ever.
Psalm 73:25-26

Folio II

The Bible

📖

These were more noble
than those in Thessalonica,
in that they received the word
with all readiness of mind,
and searched the scriptures daily,
whether those things were so.
Acts 17:11

My Bible

When I am tired, the Bible meets my need;
When I am perplexed, its wisdom great I heed.
When I am tossed, its promises I read;
When I am faint, on manna sweet I feed.

When I am sad, my Bible is my stay;
When I am afraid, it comforts me always.
When I am alone, my Bible's near at hand;
When I must fight, His Word doth give command.

When I would serve, my Bible tells me where;
When I would sing, it gives both song and air.
When I would give, the Bible tells my share;
When I would love, my Bible helps me care.

When I would run, my Bible sets the pace;
When I would pause, it shows a quiet place.
And when I yearn to see my Saviour's face,
His lovely form is outlined there in grace.

When I am old, the Bible is my friend;
When I am weak, upon it I depend.
When I must die, it blesses to the end;
All thru my life, I will its truth defend.

O blessed Book! O Word of God for me!
The Lamp from Heaven so I can clearly see!
O blessed Book! O precious book!
O Word of God that shined its beam on me.

December 1966 (music and words)

All scripture is given
by inspiration of God,
and is profitable
for doctrine, for reproof, for correction,
for instruction in righteousness:
That the man of God may be
perfect, throughly furnished
unto all good works.
2 Timothy 3:16-17

O Believe It

God has written in His Book
Great words of promise.
He has told us to believe them everyone.
They are written for our learning,
And to them we must keep turning.
Believe the precious Word of God!

God has written in His Book
Great words of comfort.
He has told us just to trust our all to Him.
They are written for our learning,
And to them we must keep turning;
Believe the precious Word of God!

God has written in His Book
Great words of wisdom.
He has told us to be wise and read His Word.
It was written for our learning,
And to it we must keep turning.
Believe the precious Word of God!

March 1962 (words set to music)

For whatsoever things were written aforetime
were written for our learning,
that we through patience and comfort
of the scriptures might have hope.
Romans 15:4

Folio II—The Bible

God's Word Is the Answer

God's Word is the answer for all of my care;
God's Word is the answer--to it I repair.
God's Word has the answer--it never will fail;
God's Word is the answer--its truth will prevail!

God's Word is the answer for all of my fears;
God's Word is the answer--it comforts and cheers.
God's Word is the answer in sickness and health;
God's Word has the answer in want or in wealth!

God's Word has the answer--it meets all my need;
God's Word has the answer, my poor soul to feed.
God's Word has the answer--it lighteth my way;
God's Word has the answer for all of my day!

God's Word has the answer for death or for life;
God's Word has the answer in triumph or strife.
God's Word has the answer in youth or old age;
God's Word has the answer on its Holy page!

March, 1965 (words set to music)

**This is my comfort in my affliction:
for thy word hath quickened me.**
Psalm 119: 50

Deep in God's Word

Deep in God's Word there are hidden
Such wonders. I gasp to behold
The purpose of God and the mysteries
The Spirit of Truth doth unfold.

Hidden behind words so common,
Yet plain to the heart that will look,
Are the treasures of Truth and His glory;
They are here in my wonderful Book.

Over and over and over again,
I read--and the pages are new;
I sing in my heart and I praise Him
And behold what the reading will do.

Old tho the same old story
The Gospel, the good news from God
It warms all my soul with its kindness,
Seeing now the dark road I once trod.

Chosen in Him and elected
Predestined, conformed to His Son
Placed in position as brethren,
With God it is already done.

Folio II—The Bible

My mind is so eager to study;
My heart is so slow to believe.
But here on the page it is written;
And the Spirit leads me to receive.

How can I ever stop seeking?
The profit is greater each day;
And I find it is Christ I discover
As I meditate, study, and pray.

I find that the fullness of Spirit
Is the fruit that God wants me to bear;
The "much fruit" which pleaseth the Father
Is Christ manifest everywhere.
His virtue, His Person, His Glory,
The Blue and the Red and the Gold,
The wonder that I am beloved--
All this in my BOOK I behold.

1945

**For whom he did foreknow,
he also did predestinate
to be conformed to the image of his Son,**
Romans 8:29

With Tears in My Heart—the Poems of Gertrude Grace Sanborn

His Wonderful Book

Deep in God's wonderful Book
Are treasures of truth for me.
Deep in God's marvelous Book,
The purpose of God I see.
I read it again and again
And its pages are ever new.
How can I ever neglect it
As I see what the reading will do?

Deep in God's wonderful Book
Are promises just for me.
Deep in His marvelous Book,
The Gospel of love I see.
It warms my poor soul with its kindness,
The message of grace so true.
Oh, I can never deny it,
But more read it thru and thru.

Deep in God's wonderful Book
I read what He's done for me.
Deep in God's wonderful Book
Are things of eternity.
The wonder that I am beloved,
The grace that has set me free--
All this and more He has written
And left in His Book for me.

1962
Written & set to original music

Folio II—The Bible

Thy Lamp

Let me hold Thy Lamp
Tho darker grows the night.
Let me hold it high
To share its perfect light.

Let me shed it forth
By word and deed each day.
Let me tell it out
Along life's busy way.

Let me hold Thy Lamp
To bear its precious flame.
Let me light some path
While speaking in Thy Name.

Let me hold Thy Lamp
And clearly show its ray
To keep the truth aglow and bright
Until I'm called away.

📖

**Thy word is a lamp unto my feet,
and a light unto my path.**
Psalms 119:105

I Did Not Read God's Word Today
A Prayer of Concern

I did not read God's Word today,
Nor did I take the time to pray;
I busy went upon my way,
And thus betrayed my Lord.

I did not lean upon His might
When new day cares came with the light;
I tried to walk by my own sight,
And thus I grieved my Lord.

I did not raise my voice in praise
But murmured oft' on many days;
And did not to myself say "nay"
And thus denied my Lord.

Dear Lord, I yearn to be so bent
Unto Thy will and be content
To trust Thee for each day and hour,
And draw from Thee Thy grace and power.

June 1969
set to music

Folio II—The Bible

My Heart's Reflection

Into a Mirror
I gazed one day;
The sight that I saw
Made me turn from my way.

I saw there myself
So vile and undone
And beheld there another
The pure Perfect One.

It was into the Book
That I looked that day;
And that which I saw
Was a heart turned away.

Compared to my Lord
To His bright Holy Light
My righteousness was
As black as the night.

Now into this Mirror
I look every day;
And, beholding, I see
My flaws fade away.

His glory I see
And He gives
Some to me
As into this Mirror I look.

2 Corinthians 3:18
1941

Thy Book

Lord, how I thank Thee
For Thy wonderful Book.
Lord, for its message
Each time I will look
Thrilling my spirit
Again and anew,
Wonderful pages
This message from you.

Lord, for its beauty
Its comfort and stay
Oh, how it helps me
Thru life's daily way,
Turning my eyes
From the world and its fare
Upon Thy promise
To cherish and care.

written in Columbus, Georgia
May 1956

Folio II—The Bible

My Wonderful Book

I sat in my place this morning;
I opened my wonderful Book;
I prayed,
"Lord, help me to read it
And believe what it said as I look!"

Each word God breathed and inspired,
Each promise and blessing so true;
Lord, help me to study the Bible
Since it is a message from you.

Thrill me; instill me with fervor
Today as I read its command.
Open my heart to God's message
When I take up God's book in my hand.

Help me to love it forever,
To lean on it, trust it always;
Teach me to reverence it always
As I sit in my place every day.

March 1984

**Thy word have I hid in mine heart,
that I might not sin against thee.**
Psalm 119:11

The Book

As I daily wash the dishes
And out my window look,
I really am not working.
I'm thinking of a Book--

A Book which had its writing
In the blood of men who died
Because they loved the author,
Jesus Christ the Crucified.

I stand and think of Moses
And of Pharaoh's wicked plot,
And think of great deliverance;
And then I think of Lot.

I praise the Lord for mercy
As it's shown down thru the age.
I say Amen while scouring
For Grace on every page.

I remember what the Book says
In Titus three and five:
That He cleansed me by the washing
And made me be alive.

So I think and wash the dishes,
And I shine up every part;
For remembering what the Book says
Brings me joy within my heart.

1940
an early attempt

Folio II—The Bible

The Prophets of Old

The prophets of old
Were courageous and bold;
They proclaimed the true message of God.
They called men to prayer
To repent everywhere
To escape from the fierce wrath of God.

They preached day by day
As they walked on their way,
And they wept as they told men their plight.
With famine and drought,
Stern lessons they taught
As they told of the Lord and His might.

So preachers today in the very same way
Call men to repent and to pray.
But they will not to hear nor His great Name revere;
And they live and they die in their sin,
While the great heart of God sends the gospel abroad
And seeks the poor lost souls to win.

June 1964

How shall they hear without a preacher?
And how shall they preach, except they be sent?
Romans 10:14-15

The Bible

Majestic, eternal, immutable BOOK
Inspired, inerrant, complete--
The Light of my path as I walk on life's way,
The Guide and the Lamp to my feet.

Its writings are holy and verbally true,
The unalterable Statute of Light,
For profit, for doctrine, for correction, reproof,
Infallible Guide to the right.

My Treasure, my Comfort, my Help, and my Stay,
Incomparable Measure and Rod,
Each page is replete with its textual proof--
The BIBLE, the exact WORD OF GOD!

September, 1979

But continue thou in the things
which thou hast learned and hast been assured of,
knowing of whom thou hast learned *them*,
and that from a child thou hast known the holy scriptures,
which are able to make thee wise unto salvation
through faith which is in Christ Jesus.
2 Timothy 3:14-15

Folio II—The Bible

The Answer

God's Word is the answer
For all of my care.
God's Word is the answer;
To It I repair.
God's Word is the answer;
He speaks to me there.
God's Word has the answer
To all of my care.

God's Word is the answer;
His promise I see.
God's Word gives me comfort
And sweet victory.
God's Word is the answer;
It lifteth my soul.
God's Word has the answer;
It maketh me whole.

God's Word gives the blessing;
It guides and It cheers.
God's Word is the answer
For all of my fears.
I thank and I praise Him
That His Word is nigh.
His Book is my statute,
My Tower so high.

Folio III

The Incarnation

And without controversy
great is the mystery of godliness:
God was manifest in the flesh,
justified in the Spirit,
seen of angels,
preached unto the Gentiles,
believed on in the world,
received up into glory.
1 Timothy 3:16

In the Fullness of Time

In the fullness of time,
God sent forth His Son,
The Seed of a woman He came;
The hope of the ages and Israel's King,
Jesus His lovely name.

Born of a virgin in Bethlehem town,
Cradled in manger's hay,
Proclaimed by the angels
Who chorused the sky
That wondrous Nativity Day.

That God so loved us
To send down His Son,
Awesome, amazing--yet true;
To offer a Saviour to save us from sin,
To save sinners like me and you.

Who gave His own life
There on Calvary's cross;
He paid the cruel price for our sin,
Now risen ascended and coming again,
This Christmas, O let Him come in!

November 1976

But when the fulness of the time was come, God sent forth his Son.
Galatians 4:4a

Folio III--The Incarnation

Jesus My Lord

Into a world aloof and cold,
The loving Saviour came
Born in a stable all alone
With nothing of rank or fame.

The poorest of shepherds beheld Him there
And cattle stood mute by His bed.
The dear Son of God was born in a barn,
And there He cradled His head.

Into the body prepared by His Lord,
He wearied and hungered and cried.
In likeness of flesh, He walked to the cross;
And there He suffered and died.

Tho dead and away three days and three nights,
The tomb could not hold God's dear Son.
He arose and ascended and now lives on high,
A proof that His work here was done.

Now living in me who believed and was saved,
Abiding and taking control,
This wonderful One, who was born in a barn,
Is my Saviour and keepeth my soul.

1945

With Tears in My Heart—the Poems of Gertrude Grace Sanborn

Marvelous Grace

Grace that He left His Home on high,
Came as a babe and born to die.

Grace that He died on Calvary's tree,
Shed His own blood as the price for me.

Grace that He rose to set me free,
Grace that He's coming back for me.

Grace, grace, God's wonderful Grace,
So rich and full and free.

Sovereign, amazing--this marvelous Grace
Which God has shown to me.

May, 1963

For the grace of God
that bringeth salvation
hath appeared to all men,
Teaching us that, denying ungodliness and worldly lusts,
we should live soberly, righteously, and godly, in this present world;
Looking for that blessed hope, and the glorious appearing
of the great God and our Saviour Jesus Christ;
Who gave himself for us, that he might redeem us from all iniquity,
and purify unto himself a peculiar people, zealous of good works.
Titus 2:11-14

Folio III--The Incarnation

Who Can Follow?

Can I follow in His footsteps?
Can I walk the road He trod?
Can I drink the cup so bitter,
Patterned by the Son of God.?

Can I say that I am guiltless
When I'm tempted like as He?
Can I keep myself as spotless
As my Lord will ever be?

Can I walk the path that He did
All the way from Bethlehem
Up the hill to cruel Golgotha,
Following the Son of Man?

I cannot follow in His footsteps!
They are perfect like as He;
I'm not saved because I follow
After Christ of Galilee.

I am saved because He died there,
And he shed His blood for me;
He was raised and lives in Heaven
Interceding there for me.

All my sin has been forgotten,
Buried deep as in the sea;
And because He went to Calvary,
God the Father seeth me.

1940

No Thought of Jesus

That time has come
With its tinsel and lights
Its hurry and getting
From morning till night.

That time comes again
With its sleigh bells and pine
With the lies about Santa
And the song and the wine.

With no thought of Jesus
God's babe in the hay
Who was sent down from Heaven
That wonderful day.

"Christmas" they call it,
But Christ they forget--
All the wonder and beauty
Of that awesome event.

This was found in handwritten form among the author's poems.
(The editor assumes it is one of her later poems.)

Folio III--The Incarnation

Ring the Bells!

Ring the bells!
And praise the Lord
That Christ was born that day.
God sent down His only Son
To in a manger lay.

Ring the bells!
Because He came
To show the world the way
To the heavenly mansion
On the cross that day.

Ring the bells!
He rose again
And never more to die.
Ring the bells!
He will return
To take His bride away.

Folio IV

The Saviour

But grow in grace,
and *in* the knowledge
of our Lord and Saviour Jesus Christ.
To him *be* glory
both now and for ever.
Amen.
2 Peter 3:18

With Tears in My Heart—the Poems of Gertrude Grace Sanborn

The Touch of Jesus

He touched the leper there that day;
He touched the dead man on the way;
He touched cold hearts to weep and pray,
The wondrous touch of Jesus.

He touched the woman with His power;
He touched the multitude that hour;
He touched the loaves and made them more,
The wondrous touch of Jesus.

He touched my heart and made me free;
He touched my eyes and made me see;
He touched my mind with liberty,
The wondrous touch of Jesus.

He touched my will and made it bend;
He touched my voice His praise to send;
He touched my soul eternally,
The wondrous touch of Jesus.

CODA:
His Holy touch
His tender touch
This touch of God in Christ for me
From Heaven to earth
From God to man
He touched us
With His great hand.

May 1962 (set to music)

Folio IV--The Saviour

He Is the Master

He is the Master I follow;
He is my Teacher and friend.
He is the Lord who will hold me
Safe and secure to the end.

He is the One only Saviour;
There's no other name to believe.
He shed His own blood there on Calvary.
Won't you repent and believe?

He is the Hope for Tomorrow;
He is the Light for Today.
He is the great Rock of Ages;
O come and receive Him today.

📖

**And why call ye me, Lord, Lord,
and do not the things which I say?**
Luke 6:46

Wonderful Saviour

Wonderful, wonderful Saviour
Perfect salvation He gives;
Constant and blessed assurance
Wonderful presence within.
Abiding joy in His service
Wonderful privilege to go;
Wonderful gospel to tell all the world
Wonderful message to know.

Wonderful beautiful promise,
Jesus will come in the air;
Wonderful, blessed bright prospect,
Release from trials and care.
Wonderful bliss when I see Him,
Wonderful Home in the sky;
Wonderful years with Jesus my Lord,
Living and reigning on high.

Wonderful, wonderful Saviour
Teaching me right from the wrong;
Wonderful, wonderful Saviour
Giving my life a new song.
Wonderful, wonderful Saviour
Keeping me steadfast within;
Wonderful Grace of Jesus my Lord
Wonderful freedom from sin.

Folio IV--The Saviour

Wonderful, Wonderful Jesus

Once I was lost and a child of sin;
All of my bent was away from Him.
But He redeemed me and took me in;
Wonderful, wonderful Jesus!

When in time past but a child of wrath,
He set my feet on His righteous path.
And I am now bound for the Home He hath--
Wonderful, wonderful Jesus!

Never to fall from His hands so strong;
Never alone tho my way be long.
How can I help but to sing this song--
Wonderful, wonderful Jesus!

O to give praise to His matchless name,
Always unchanging and just the same--
Wonderful Lord and wonderful name,
Wonderful Lord, Christ Jesus!

June 1961 (set to music)

📖

For by grace are ye saved through faith;
and that not of yourselves:
***it is* the gift of God:**
Not of works, lest any man should boast.
Ephesians 2:8-9

A Simple Song

When I behold His perfect face
All thru the Book
Shown there in grace,
I lift this heart in glad refrain
And sing a song to Him again.

O may I ever long to see
His likeness manifest in me,
That I may show this world of sin
That God's dear Son
Doth reign within.

I long to please Him more and more
And lay before Him my heart's store
Of adoration and of praise,
And live for Him thru all my days.

O vast and mighty is the plan
That brought salvation down to man;
How past my mind its scope and love
Drawn from the pit to Heaven above.

1945

Folio IV--The Saviour

Rafters of Fir

The beams of His house are of cedar;
The rafters above it are fir.
Evergreen with the fragrance of living,
His building will ever endure.

His church has its strength in its builder;
The beams and the rafters are sure.
And no one can ever destroy it;
As Himself, it must ever endure.

He died on the Tree to secure it
And is risen above holding fast.
All the rafters of fir of His building
And the beams, which are cedar, will last.

August 1962

> The beams
> of our house
> are cedar,
> and our rafters
> of fir.

Song of Solomon 1:17

He Is the Master

He is the Master I follow;
He is my Teacher and friend.
He is the Lord who will hold me
Safe and secure to the end.

He is the One only Saviour;
There's no other name to believe.
He shed His own blood there on Calvary;
Won't you repent and believe?

He is the Hope for Tomorrow;
He is the Light for Today.
He is the great Rock of Ages;
O come and receive Him today.

*Neither is there salvation in any other:
for there is none other name
under heaven
given among men,
whereby we must be saved.*
Acts 4:12

Folio IV--The Saviour

Consider Him

He alone is worthy of our trusting;
Touched is He with every grief and pain.
He rebukes with perfect, Holy knowledge;
He tries oft' that we might patience gain.

He alone can make earthly ties grow fainter;
Only He can make world-lure fade away.
He alone--none but Christ consider
As we journey on this pilgrim way.

Perhaps 1944

For we have not an high priest
which cannot be touched
with the feeling of our infirmities;
but was in all points tempted
like as *we are*,
yet without sin.
Let us therefore come boldly
unto the throne of grace,
that we may obtain mercy,
and find grace
to help in time of need.
Hebrews 4:15-16

Wonderful Salvation

Wonderful salvation
That brought me in relation
To the God of Glory
And Jesus Christ His Son.

Gave to me a teacher,
Showing me each feature
Of the spotless life
Of Jesus Christ His Son.

Makes me want to praise Him,
And spend eternal days in
Telling forth the story
Of redeeming love.

Glory to the Spirit,
His Word He makes me hear it
All because He saved me
By Jesus Christ His Son.

1946

**Neither is there salvation in any other:
for there is none other name under heaven given among men,
whereby we must be saved.**
Acts 4:12

Folio IV--The Saviour

'Tis My Lord

Men and books
May come and go,
But 'tis my Lord
That I love so.
Words and plans
Of might and vim,
Cannot e'en compare
With Him.
Songs and hymns
And oratory
Only faintly
Tell His Glory.
Teachers, preachers,
Men of fame,
Try but simply
Grace His Name.

1946

Thou shalt love the Lord thy God
with all thy heart,
and with all thy soul,
and with all thy mind.
This is the first and great commandment.
Matthew 22:37-38

No Place to Hide

The people are seeking a shelter
To hide from the missiles and bombs,
But there's no place to hide
But in Jesus
There is no place to hide
But in Him.

There's no place to hide
But in the Saviour.
There's no place to hide
But in His care.
There's no place to hide
In all this world wide,
No shelter or rock anywhere.

There's no place to hide
But in His keeping.
No Name to hold Who guards or keeps
There's no place to hide
But in the Saviour
No place, no place,
No place to hide.

October, 1962
During threatened Cuban invasion

Folio IV--The Saviour

Praise

O Jesus, I love Thee
Because Thou art fair.
Because of Thy beauty
With which none can compare.

O Master, I love Thee
Because Thou art strong.
Because of The power,
I'm kept all day long.

O Saviour, I love Thee
Because Thou didst die;
Because Thou hast saved me
Though sinful am I.

I praise Thee and hale Thee
Thou blest Three in One.
I long to be with Thee
When this life is done.

Chorus:
O Blessed and Holy One, Wonderful Lord
O precious and cleansing, inspiring Word

1940

Let Me See Jesus

Let me see Jesus
My wonderful Lord;
Let me see Jesus
When I read His Word.

Show me His beauty;
Show me His grace;
Wonderful portrait
Of His lovely face.

Let me see Calv'ry;
There I shall see
How much it cost Him
My Saviour to be.

1964 (words are set to music)

**And when they had lifted up their eyes,
they saw no man, save Jesus only.**
Matthew 17:8

Folio IV--The Saviour

Safe in His Hands

In His hands safe,
Kept, and secure;
Safe from the perils of life,
Nothing can sever.
Nothing can change Him--
Neither sorrow or danger or strife.

His strong, tender hands
That direct every day
Molding this clay to His will,
Transforming my life
Conformed to His Son,
If I submit to His will.

In such hands I am kept--
His strong, sovereign hands,
Which made the earth and the sky.
Why should I fear or wonder at all
If I may live or may die?

My times *are* in thy hand:
deliver me from the hand of mine enemies,
and from them that persecute me.
Psalm 31:15

Folio V

The Shepherd

Now the God of peace,
that brought again from the dead
our Lord Jesus,
that great shepherd of the sheep,
through the blood of the everlasting covenant,
Make you perfect in every good work to do his will,
working in you that which is wellpleasing in his sight,
through Jesus Christ;
to whom *be* glory
for ever and ever. Amen.
Hebrews 13:20-21

My Shepherd Forever

The Lord is my Shepherd forever;
He leadeth me day by day.
By streams of cool waters, He leads me;
Revives me along my way.

The Lord is my Shepherd forever;
He guideth me every day.
Thru valleys of sorrow and trials,
He lovingly leads the way.

The Lord is my Shepherd I follow
Both when I am young or am old;
He faithfully holds me forever
And shelters me in His dear fold.

The Lord is my Shepherd forever;
He's there by my side night and day.
In sunshine and shadow, He leads me
And guides lest I go astray.

The Lord is my Shepherd;
So loving and tender is He.
The Lord is my Shepherd forever,
For now and eternity.

1970 (words and music)

Folio IV—The Shepherd

Tho other voices speak to me,
I know His voice the best.
For no one else knows me as well
Or keeps my heart at rest.

The Shepherd is my Saviour,
Great Tender of His sheep;
And from the dead will raise me
Who trusts in Him to keep.

Yea, I will ever praise Him,
This Bishop of my soul;
This great and Holy Leader
Precedes me to my goal.

June 1961 (set to music)

📖

For ye were
as sheep
going astray;
but are now returned
unto the Shepherd and Bishop
of your souls.
1 Peter 2:25

The Lord Is My Shepherd

The Lord is my shepherd;
Not one thing I need.
In His green pastures,
I safely may feed.

Beside His still waters,
My soul finds its rest.
He leadeth me onward,
And He knoweth best.

Through the Valley of Shadow
Though death seeks its prey,
Surely goodness and mercy
Goes with me all way.

A table before me
He sets here below;
And there in sweet blessing
His presence I know.

My head He anointeth
With peace for my mind;
How wise is my shepherd
How tender, how kind.

Folio IV—The Shepherd

The Skillful Shepherd

Wherever He goeth
The sheep that He knoweth
Will follow the Lamb.
The Shepherd He giveth
The life each one liveth
For He is "I Am."

Fresh pastures He leadeth
Them into, and feedeth
The sheep of His hand.
He skillfully guideth
To where He abideth,
The Heavenly land.

1962

My sheep hear my voice,
and I know them,
and they follow me:
And I give unto them eternal life;
and they shall never perish,
neither shall any man
pluck them out of my hand.
John 10:27-28

My Saviour Is My Shepherd

My Saviour is my Shepherd;
I neither want nor need.
And in His pleasant pastures
By waters still I feed.

A table sweet He has prepared
Of fellowship sublime.
And on my mind His peace He pours
And heals me every time.

In paths of service He doth lead
And never leads astray--
Though we walk thru shadows,
Or death makes me His prey.

Surely He will care for me
The whole long journey thru.
His mercy follows like a guard;
His goodness follows too.

His rod and staff they keep me true
By comfort and restraint.
Lest on this thorny path I fall
Or being weary faint.

Folio IV—The Shepherd

The Lord is my shepherd;
He tendeth His sheep.
And not one doth wander
From His mighty keep.

In The House of the Lord,
I will dwell all my days.
The Lord is my shepherd;
To Him I give praise!

June 1964 (set to music)

📖

The LORD *is* my shepherd; I shall not want.
He maketh me to lie down in green pastures:
he leadeth me beside the still waters.
He restoreth my soul:
he leadeth me in the paths of righteousness for his name's sake.
Yea, though I walk through the valley of the shadow of death,
I will fear no evil: for thou *art* with me; thy rod & thy staff they comfort me.
Thou preparest a table before me in the presence of mine enemies:
thou anointest my head with oil; my cup runneth over.
Surely goodness and mercy shall follow me all the days of my life:
and I will dwell in the house of the LORD for ever.
Psalm 23

Folio VI

Calvary

And when they were come
to the place, which is called Calvary,
there they crucified him, and the malefactors,
one on the right hand, and the other on the left.
Then said Jesus, Father, forgive them;
for they know not what they do.
Luke 23:33-34

With Tears in My Heart—the Poems of Gertrude Grace Sanborn

Calvary

Calvary, that Holy Hill of pain
Where Jesus bled and died for me;
Calvary, that place of guilt and shame
Where on the cross He set me free.

Calvary, those bleeding wounds I see,
That crown of thorns His agony;
How can I be the same
Since I have learned the name
Of Calvary?

August 1966
The author wrote this for Calvary Baptist Church in Gulfport, Florida.
(The author also wrote beautiful music to go with these words.)

Folio VI--Calvary

Amazing Truth

Amazing Truth
That He should die
And give His life for me
To bear my sin upon the cross
And pay the penalty.

Amazing Truth
That God's own Son
Did lay His glory by
And come to take
The form of man
So on the cross to die.

Amazing Truth
He's coming back
To take His Church away
To be with Him for evermore
Thru God's own endless day.

Amazing Truth
Amazing Grace
That He should die for me.

February 1964
This poem is set to music.

Though He Was Rich

Though He was rich, yet for me
He became poor
And died on the Tree for me.
Though He was rich, yet for me
He gave His all
That I might be rich as He.

He came to dwell in the form
Of sinful men,
And suffered and died for me.
Though He was Lord, yet He stooped
Servant to be
And paid all my penalty.

Though He was rich, yet for me
He became poor
And left His great throne above.
Though poor was I, yet He died,
Made me an heir,
And paid such a price in love.

Chorus:
O wondrous love
That He should give himself;
O wondrous grace
That He should die.
How can it be that one so rich as He
Would spend His all
For such as I?

1964 (The author set these words to music)

Folio VI--Calvary

On to Calvary

E'en from the womb of the virgin
And from the manger's hay,
Straight from the cradle to Calvary
Jesus was pressed on His way.

Naught of this world could deter Him,
Neither sickness nor demon nor man;
Steadfast His face set toward Calvary,
Straightened to fulfill God's plan.

Mocked and reviled and mistreated,
Forsaken by even His own,
He steadfastly walked on to Calvary;
Ah, He went to Calvary alone.

He willingly hung there a ransom
And offered His life's blood for me;
In Him all Scripture was honored,
And there He fulfilled prophecy.

Out of the glory of Heaven
And into this world of woe,
Came He with eyes then on Calvary
And onward to Calvary did go.

Wonderful, faithful Lord Jesus,
Leaving such Glory for me
To purchase a ransom on Calv'ry.
O what a Saviour is He!

1949 (after a personal study in the Gospel of Luke)

He Found Me

When I was walking along life's way
Living for self in every way,
Having no thought I was lost in sin,
Knowing not Jesus would take me in.

Aimlessly drifting along life's sea,
Wasting my time in mirth and glee,
Having no thought of a better way,
Knowing not God had provided a Way.

No one had told me of Calvary,
No one had said He died for me,
No one explained to me there was more
Than this poor world with its passing store.

Then He sought me, He found me, He saved me,
He lifted me out of my sin.
He loved me, He drew me, He saved me,
In marvelous grace took me in.

He sought me, He found me, He saved me,
And gave me a deep joy within,
My heart now will praise Him forever,
For He found me and saved me from sin.

1970 (words set to music by the author)

Folio VI--Calvary

Surely

"Surely," said the Book, "He carried my sorrows."
"Surely," said the Word, "He bore my griefs."
"Surely," said the Lord, "I'm coming quickly."
Precious Lord, help Thou mine unbelief.

📖

> Surely he hath borne our griefs,
> and carried our sorrows:
> yet we did esteem him stricken,
> smitten of God, and afflicted.
> *Isaiah 53:4,*

> He which testifieth these things saith,
> Surely I come quickly. Amen.
> Even so, come, Lord Jesus.
> *Revelation 22:20*

A Cross on a Hill

I read in God's Word of a Cross on a hill
Where wicked ones nailed Him one day.
I read how they mocked Him and spit on His face;
Then brutally led Him away.

I saw where they nailed Him upon a cruel Tree;
I saw the two thieves by His side.
I saw how they hung Him on Golgotha's hill;
I read how He bled there and died.

I saw the rent vail as the sun hid His face;
I heard His great cry as He died.
I saw there my Saviour Who bore all my sin;
And for me was there crucified.

My heart is so stirred as I learned from God's Word
The price that He paid on that Tree.
O Lord, melt my heart
As I see there His Blood
Which He shed while on dark Calvary!

Folio VI--Calvary

The Blood of His Cross

The Blood of His cross--
O how precious and holy!
It covers the sin
Of the lost, guilty one.

It avails for the souls
Of our innocent children
And those who are sick
And weak and undone.

The Blood of His cross--
That blest cleansing flow--
We are by its crimson
Made whiter than snow.

It availeth forever;
Its power will abide.
That life-stream from Calvary
That flowed from His side.

📖

And, having made peace through the blood of his cross, by him to reconcile all things unto himself; by him, *I say*, whether *they be* things in earth, or things in heaven.
Colossians 1:20

Folio VII

Christ's Session

Wherefore he is able also to save them to the uttermost
that come unto God by him,
seeing he ever liveth to make intercession for them.
For such an high priest became us,
who is holy, harmless, undefiled, separate from sinners,
and made higher than the heavens;
Who needeth not daily, as those high priests, to offer up sacrifice,
first for his own sins, and then for the people's:
for this he did once, when he offered up himself.
Hebrews 7:25-27

My Great High Priest

I have a friend;
He's seated in the Heavenlies,
One who is touched
With all my need and cares.
Ascended up,
He's there beside the Father;
I have a friend who watches my affairs.

My Risen Lord
Has entered in before me;
Within the vail
My Surety abides.
And if I fail,
My Advocate defends me
Before the face of God what e'er betide.

I'm not alone;
He never leaves me.
His wondrous grace
Supplies my every need.
My great High Priest
Has entered in before me;
Before the throne, my very case doth plead.

VII—Christ's Session

My great High Priest
Is seated in the Heavenlies;
His tender eye is over all my care;
His loving heart is touched
With my infirmity,
My great High Priest who hears
My faintest prayer.

📖

For we have not an high priest
which cannot be touched
with the feeling of our infirmities;
but was in all points tempted like as we are,
yet without sin.
Let us therefore come boldly
unto the throne of grace,
that we may obtain mercy,
and find grace to help in time of need.
Hebrews 4:15-16

Wondrous Love

In the far off Heaven
On the Father's throne
Sits my Lord and Saviour
Keeping fast His own.

His by right of purchase,
The price His precious blood--
All this overwhelms me
Like a mighty flood.

Long ago He bought me,
And then in Love He sought me.
This the Spirit taught me,
Wondrous, wondrous love.

March 1946
set to music in 1961

Ye were ... redeemed ...
with the precious blood of Christ,
as of a lamb without blemish and without spot:
1 Peter 1:18-19

VII—Christ's Session

God's A B C's

A is for Adam who did not obey.
B is for Blood which washed sin away.
C is for Care God gives great and small.
D is for Daniel the bravest of all.
E is for Ever, the Work which He starts.
F is for Faith which He puts in our hearts.
G is for Grace so full and so free.
H is for Home preparing for me.
I is for In the door and then out.
J is for Judgment with trumpet and shout.
K is for Kingdom when Jesus shall reign.
L is for Looking, He's coming again.
M is for Mystery, the dead shall be raised.
N is for No where, where he can't be praised.
O is for Only, the one God is He.
P is for Perfect and holy to be.
Q is for Quicken, alive and awake.
R is for Righteousness, our garment He makes.
S is for Saviour Who died for our sins.
T is for Telling some others to win.
U is for Under His wings to abide.
V is for Victory and to walk by His side.
W is for Worship and Waiting and Word.
X is a letter that seldom is heard.
Y is for Yesterday, today, and for ever.
Z is for Zealous in gathering together.

Folio VIII

Christ's Second Coming

Beloved, now are we the sons of God,
and it doth not yet appear what we shall be:
but we know that, when he shall appear,
we shall be like him; for we shall see him as he is.
And every man that hath this hope in him
purifieth himself, even as he is pure.
1 John 3:2-3

Jesus Is Coming

Jesus is coming;
It may not be long.
Jesus is coming;
Let this be your song.

Jesus is coming;
O let us rejoice.
Jesus is coming;
O lift up your voice.

Jesus is coming;
It may be this hour.
Proclaim the gospel
Once more in its power.

Jesus is coming;
O Christian prepare.
O come, Lord Jesus;
For this is my prayer.

1967

Folio VIII—Christ's Second Coming

Till He Come

Till He come,
I will remember
How He gave Himself for me,
Gave Himself a willing ransom
On the cross of Calvary.

Till He come,
O blessed privilege
To partake of wine and bread,
Bring to mind our dear Redeemer
Now alive who once was dead.

Till He come,
As oft' ye do it,
Worship Him His will obey;
Come together, saints below here,
Till He calls His Bride away.

Till He come,
And so examine
At His gracious table sit
Washed and cleansed to wait before Him,
Grace that He has ordered it.

1943

**For as often as ye eat this bread, and drink this cup,
ye do shew the Lord's death till he come.**
1 Corinthians 11:26

How Can I Wait?

How can I wait?
It seems so long to see Him.
How can I wait
To see His lovely face?

How can I wait
To hear His voice so beautiful?
How can I wait?
So cries my yearning heart.

How can I wait?
Yet His Word spurs me on.
How can I wait?
Yet, He alone doth know the time!

June 1961 (words set to music)

**For the earnest expectation
of the creature
waiteth for the manifestation
of the sons of God.**
Romans 8:19;

Folio VIII—Christ's Second Coming

Jesus Is Coming Again

Sometimes my heart is sad;
Sometimes the way seems long.
Sometimes the shadows fall;
Sometimes I have no song.
But when I read His Word,
How my heart is stirred;
For He is coming--is coming again!

Wars and their rumors may come,
Kingdoms may wax and wane,
Rulers may rise and fall,
Wicked men gain acclaim;
But when I read His Word,
O how my heart is stirred;
For He is coming--is coming again!

September, 1964

Behold, I shew you a mystery;
We shall not all sleep,
but we shall all be changed,
In a moment, in the twinkling of an eye,
at the last trump: for the trumpet shall sound,
and the dead shall be raised incorruptible,
and we shall be changed.
1 Corinthians 15:51-52

With Tears in My Heart—the Poems of Gertrude Grace Sanborn

Expectation

My heart doth wait;
My Lord will soon be coming.
My heart doth wait
To see His lovely face.
My heart doth wait
To hear His voice so beautiful.
For His return
So longs my yearning heart.
My heart doth wait;
This song, keeps ringing on.
He's coming soon,
And this thought spurs me on.
For Him I wait,
But He alone doth know the time.
My heart doth wait and sings its song.
He's coming soon;
He's coming soon.
My heart doth wait;
My heart doth wait.

1961 (words and music)

**My soul, wait thou only upon God;
for my expectation *is* from him.**
Psalms 62:5

Folio VIII—Christ's Second Coming

I Cannot Wait

I cannot wait;
It seems so long to see Him.
I cannot wait
To see His lovely face.

I cannot wait
To hear His voice so beautiful.
I cannot wait
So yearns my longing heart.

I cannot wait;
This song keeps ringing in me.
I cannot wait;
'Tis the thought that spurs me on.

I cannot wait;
He alone doth know the time.
I cannot wait;
It won't be long!

I cannot wait!
I cannot wait!

Romans 8:19, Song of Solomon 2:5, 8, 14
June, 1961 (set to music)

For the earnest expectation of the creature waiteth for the manifestation of the sons of God.
Romans 8:19

These Things I Know

These things I know,
O praise His name;
These things I know,
While trials here perplex me so.

I know He lives and does not sleep
And that His arm is strong to keep.
I know His Word will last for aye
Tho men and things will pass away.

I know He saved me by His grace
And promised I shall see His face.
I know He's coming back some day
To catch His longing Bride away.

I know that when earth's journey's done,
The battle o'er the victory won,
That I in heaven will find my place
Close by His side in His embrace.
These things I know.

December 1951

For I know whom I have believed, and am persuaded that he is able to keep that which I have committed unto him against that day.
2 Timothy 1:12

Folio VIII—Christ's Second Coming

It May Be Today

One day, and it may be today,
We shall hear His great commanding shout.
And while we are busy at our tasks,
He will come to take us out

"Come up, come up hither!"
And, in a moment--"a twinkling"--It will be.
We shall be with Him
Whom we so long have yearned to see.

With wondrous joy, we shall hear his voice
Which bids the dead to rise and leave earth's shroud.
Our dear, dear dead that we have missed so long
They rise in beauty to meet us in the cloud.

Fulfilled His promise, we'll rise
And leave behind earth's tears and fears--
The things we could not understand or comprehend
To be together with Him, eternal years.

To be with Him, wherever that may be,
Our glorious Lord, in His blest company.
So let us wait and sing hope's sweetest song;
One day! Hold fast! It won't be long.

Folio IX

Christian Service

I beseech you therefore, brethren,
by the mercies of God,
that ye present your bodies a living sacrifice,
holy, acceptable unto God, *which is* your reasonable service.
And be not conformed to this world:
but be ye transformed by the renewing of your mind,
that ye may prove what *is* that good,
and acceptable, and perfect, will of God.
Romans 12:1-2

Grace

Hard is the pathway of training,
Stern is the way He may use
To take our dim eyes from the earth things,
To make us His own will to choose.

How often our hands seem to cling to
The baubles and toys of this sphere,
But a wonderful wise overseer
Will give us of things far more dear.

He seats us in Heavenly places,
Enfolds us around with His care,
Bestows on us gifts for His glory
That we may be used everywhere.

He lets us see failure in others,
Permits us to weep over loss,
And does all this while He is turning
Our eyes from this world to His cross.

April, 1953

And he said unto me, My grace is sufficient for thee:
for my strength is made perfect in weakness.
Most gladly therefore will I rather glory in my infirmities,
that the power of Christ may rest upon me.
2 Corinthians 12:9

Folio IX—Christian Service

The Cost

Little did I know
The day I gave to Him my all
The cost of such surrender
Or the meaning of His call.

My plans, my thoughts, my talents,
And my children did I bring;
And I laid them on the Altar
For my Lord and Heavenly King.

He accepted them from me
For I gladly placed them there;
Then He began to use me
And the children that I bare.

Ah, not in place of honor
Or high favor, or acclaim;
But He gently made us lowly
Thus to magnify His name.

No foreign shores of glamour
No fame in public place;
He used us in our weakness
While clinging to His Grace.

How lightly some do answer
When He asks them for their all.
How little do they reckon
On the cost of such a call.

1951

Whosoever doth not bear his cross, & come after me, cannot be my disciple.
Luke 14:27

I Know Not!

I know not,
But He knoweth;
He knoweth the way
To go or to stay;
He knoweth each day.

I know not,
But He knoweth;
He knoweth the plan
And each willing man;
He knoweth, He can.

I know not,
But He knoweth;
He knoweth the cost
To go to the lost;
He paid it for me.

I know not,
But He knoweth;
He heareth my cry;
And when I do sigh,
He knoweth just why.

I know not,
But He knoweth;
He knoweth my need
And has promised to lead
If I sow the seed.

1959

Folio IX—Christian Service

Don't Let Your Vision Grow Dim

Don't let your vision grow dim;
Don't tire of the toil and the task.
Don't let the cost of your heavenly call
Keep you from following Him.

Don't let the vision grow dim;
Don't let your purpose grow faint.
Don't let the yearnings recede from your heart;
Don't let your vision grow dim.

Don't let your vision grow dim;
Don't let the fire burn low.
Forget not the plight of those souls lost in sin;
Don't let your vision grow dim.

1967

And let us not be weary
in well doing:
for in due season
we shall reap,
if we faint not.
Galatians 6:9

With Tears in My Heart—the Poems of Gertrude Grace Sanborn

Faithful to the Fight

Faithful to the fight
Faithful to the faith
Faithful to the finish for God.

Faithful to the right
Faithful to His might
Faithful to the Word of God.

Faithful in the fray
Faithful every day
Faithful in the fight for the faith.

Faithful to the fight
Faithful to the faith
Faithful to the finish for God.

The author wrote this while a member of Calvary Baptist Church in Gulfport, Florida. The pastor of that church had always said: "Be faithful to the fight, faithful to the faith, and faithful to the finish for God." Her church sang this chorus often as a theme song. She dedicated this gospel chorus to her son-in-law, D. A. Waite.

📖

**I have fought a good fight,
I have finished *my* course,
I have kept the faith:**
2 Timothy 4:7

Folio IX—Christian Service

The Field of God's Harvest

The field of God's Harvest is vast and wide;
Yet each must serve in his place.
The Lord of the Harvest has planned it well,
And provides a supply of grace.

All over the world brave servants proclaim
And show forth the true message of love;
Knowing full well when the telling is o'er,
They must give a report up above.

Sometimes it may seem they serve quite alone
And the enemy's weapons too strong;
But God's in His heaven surveying it all,
So press on for it won't be long.

So keep to the task, to the work, to the fray,
Not counting the heartache and loss.
For He was not willing that any should perish;
And for this He went to the cross.

June 1960

📖

**Pray ye therefore the Lord of the harvest,
that he will send forth labourers into his harvest.**
Matthew 9:38

Mine Eyes Have Seen the King

Mine eyes have seen the King;
He impels me, "Go!"
Mine eyes have seen the King;
I dare not tell Him, "No!"
Mine eyes have seen the King;
I answered, "Here, Lord, am I!"

March 1965

I saw also the Lord sitting upon a throne,
high and lifted up, and his train filled the temple.
Above it stood the seraphims: . . .
And one cried unto another, and said,
Holy, holy, holy, *is* the LORD of hosts:
the whole earth *is* full of his glory.
And the posts of the door moved at the voice of him that cried,
and the house was filled with smoke.
Then said I, Woe *is* me! for I am undone;
because I *am* a man of unclean lips,
and I dwell in the midst of a people of unclean lips:
for mine eyes have seen the King, the LORD of hosts.

Isaiah 6:1-5

Folio IX—Christian Service

My All Today

All that I am or want to be
I must be for Him today,
Serving Him now
With all of my heart
While there is time to stay.

All of my life, my strength, my love
I must live out for Him while I may.
For only the present
Is mine to give;
Tomorrow may call me away.

January 1956

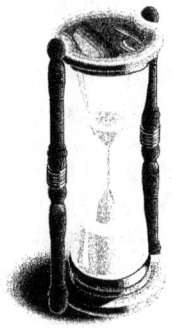

I Would Not Step into This Care

I would not step
Into this care
Nor long to learn
Some lesson there.
But if God's hand doth place me here,
I will not mourn
To be elsewhere.

Tho stern the test with tear or sigh,
I'll trust His grace
Nor even try
To leave my care to run away.
For though 'tis rough,
He leads the way.

I would not step into this care
Nor long to learn
Some lesson there.
But willingly I take my stand
Within the place
Of His command.

February 1965

**We know that all things work together for good
to them that love God,**
Romans 8:28

Folio IX—Christian Service

Set Your Heart

Set your heart to the Lord
As a clock to the sun;
Follow His leading
Till your hard day is done.

Set your heart to the Lord;
Keep looking to Him
No matter the trial,
Though the tears may be dim.

Set your heart to the Lord
And on His Word be stayed;
Believe what is written
And trust His right way.

Set your affection
on things
above,
not
on things
on the earth.
Colossians 3:2

Living for Jesus

Living for Jesus and walking His way
Living for Jesus each hour of the day
Living for Jesus and telling His praise
Living for Jesus thru all of my days.

Living for Jesus in joy and in tears
Living for Jesus until He appears
Living for Jesus for soon He will come
Living for Jesus to hear His "well done."

Living for Jesus my wonderful Lord
Living for Jesus believing His word
Living for Jesus my wonderful friend
Living for Jesus right unto the end.

November, 1964

Folio IX—Christian Service

Shut-in

Shut-in for love,
That's what I say.
What matter I stay here
Day after day?

Shut-in to serve
Those who rely,
Hearing and answering
Their precious weak cry.

Shut-in for love,
Day after day;
With each service I give,
I look up and pray!

Shut-in with loving
Those clinging to me;
O teach me such leaning
And clinging to Thee!

Lord of the "shut-ins,"
Stay close by my side
And give me a song
Whatever betide!

1977

Whithersoever

"Whithersoever,"
I heard Him call,
And so I replied:
"I give my all."

"Reflect on your answer,"
He spoke at the start.
For He knew the breach
Twixt my words and my heart.

So He led, and I followed
Thru each waiting day
Till my heart and words
Had but one voice to say,
"Whithersoever!"

August 1952
This poem was written after the Sunday morning sermon by Pastor Earl V.
Willetts at Berea Baptist Church in Berea, Ohio. Mrs. Sanborn's daughter
Audrey died the following November.

> As they went in the way,
> a certain man said unto him,
> Lord, I will follow thee
> whithersoever thou goest.
> *Luke 9:57*

Folio IX—Christian Service

Do It Unto Him

Do it unto the Lord for He understands;
Do it all to His name and be blessed.
No matter if others regard it as small,
No matter if anyone sees it at all.
Do it unto the Lord.

Do it unto the Lord; He knoweth your strength;
He knoweth each effort and seeth each length.
He watches each testing and appraiseth the cause;
He lists our endurance and maketh each pause.
Do it unto the Lord.

Do it unto the Lord; it bringeth sweet peace,
A balm for aloneness and wondrous release.
He measures our lack and He knoweth our frame;
And He giveth contentment when it's done in His name.
Do it unto the Lord.

February 1954

Verily I say unto you,
Inasmuch as ye have done *it*
unto one of the least of these my brethren,
ye have done *it* unto me.
Matthew 25:40

Remain In Your Place

If you're discontented and unhappy
And your place and purpose grows dim,
There is always a ship at Joppa
If you don't want to stay and win.

If you turn from the task of the present
To follow a beckoning star,
There is always a ship at Joppa
To take you from where you are.

But you'll miss the blessing He gives you
If you wander away from His place;
For there's a fare to be paid at Joppa
If you do not remain in your place.

November 1983
This was written when a beloved pastor considered a move to another church.

Folio IX—Christian Service

Perhaps

Perhaps He has for you a place
Where you may show His special grace;
A place where trust quite pure and sweet
May be displayed in rest complete.
And at this place, He has some soul
Whom you may comfort and console--
Someone alone, afraid, and sad
That you can by your faith make glad
Because you suffered once and wept,
But did His way and will accept.
So in your present place of trial,
Cling to the Father all the while.
Believe the Word; He cares for you
And has some work that you can do.

1953

Blessed be . . . the God of all comfort;
Who comforteth us in all our tribulation,
that we may be able to comfort
them which are in any trouble,
by the comfort
wherewith we ourselves
are comforted of God.
2 Corinthians 1:3-4

The Burning Bush

Moses saw the burning bush,
And turned aside to behold it.
Today there is nothing outstanding or supernatural
About a bush which is on fire.
We see forest fires everyday;
But to see a continuous fire
Which burns on and on is unusual.
Most every Christian has some love
For the things of the Lord,
And does--for a time--flame out
In true spiritual fire for God;
But to behold a believer who is continually "burning"
Thru sickness and sadness,
And in poverty or loss--
Yes, even in joy or abundance--
Is indeed a sight to "turn aside" and behold.
We take our shoes off before such Holy Ground,
For this is truly Christ having His way in us.

1958 (an original meditation)
The author wrote, " Lord help me to be a bush--continual burning."

God called unto him out of the midst of the bush . . . and he said,
Draw not nigh hither: put off thy shoes from off thy feet,
for the place whereon thou standest *is* holy ground.

Exodus 3:4-5

Folio IX—Christian Service

None of These Things

But none of these things move me;
Neither count I my life dear
So that I may run my course with joy
And complete my service here.

But none of these things move me,
So sufficient is His grace
To proclaim the gospel daily
Until I shall see His face.
March 1965

But none of these things move me,
neither count I my life dear unto myself,
so that I might finish my course with joy,
and the ministry,
which I have received
of the Lord Jesus,
to testify the gospel
of the grace of God.
Acts 20:24

Endure Hardness

Endure hardness!
As a soldier good.
Stand at your post
As a soldier should!

Eyes to the right!
With Sword out of sheath.
Ready to march
If the Leader should speak!

Endure Hardness!
Tho stern be your pace,
Serve without murmur
In the soldier's place!

1981

**Thou therefore endure hardness,
as a good soldier
of Jesus Christ.**
2 Timothy 2:3

Folio IX—Christian Service

A Song

I had a song within my heart
When Jesus saved me.
I have it still
Though there've been tears and fears.

I have it yet,
Though I am growing older.
I'll have it always,
No matter come the years.

I have that song,
'Tis sweeter far and dearer,
Of grace and peace
And His sustaining power.

And if I weep or falter
In my singing,
It's for the days I've wasted
And the hours.

📖

**Let the word of Christ dwell in you richly in all wisdom;
teaching & admonishing one another in psalms &hymns & spiritual songs,
singing with grace in your hearts to the Lord.**
Colossians 3:16

Folio X

God's Will

For so is the will of God,
that with well doing ye may put to silence the ignorance of foolish men:
1 Peter 2:15

Love not the world, neither the things *that are* in the world.
If any man love the world, the love of the Father is not in him.
For all that *is* in the world, the lust of the flesh, and the lust of the eyes, and
the pride of life, is not of the Father, but is of the world.
And the world passeth away, and the lust thereof:
but he that doeth the will of God abideth for ever.
1 John 2:15-17

'Tis His Will

I do not know what lies ahead;
I only know
I need not dread.

I do not know of joy or pain
Or if may be a loss or gain
If 'tis His will for me.

I do not know how it can be
That trials hard are best for me,
Yet 'tis His way for me.

I do not know how I can sing
Except that God's in everything,
And He will strengthen me.

I do not need to fret or cry
Or need to ever wonder why
If 'tis His will for me.

1977

Folio X—God's Will

When God Closes the Door

When God closes doors,
It is because
He knows what is behind them.
He shelters as He leads;
We cannot see the trials
Thru its portals
But only glimpse the duty
That we need.

He may permit a look in thru an archway
To show us there
What someday we may do;
Or let us view
With eyes of reverent wonder
What we've escaped
By our not going thru.

But God is wise;
Indeed, His Name is Wisdom;
Just trust Him then;
Be strong and do not faint.
For when all things
Are ready in His purpose,
A door will open wide
With no restraint.

July 1960

The Closed Door

The closed door
Seemed good and full of store;
Yet better far
That He should bar
Each door that seemed so free and due,
Lest we go boldly walking thru
And find there only tears
Far greater than our present fears.

Do you face
What seems a narrow place?
No leading still;
Yet, we must learn His will.
How can I go astray,
For there He stands and blocks the way.
To Him I would be true
In everything I seek to do.

Lord, teach me
To trust; and help me see
To wait is best.
For I must have the test,
Lest I may yearn for fame
And bring dishonor to Thy Name
Or may Thy Word forget
And all my years have deep regret.

Folio X—God's Will

How much He cares that He will bar
What seems a bright and shining star,
For we would go most anywhere
Unless He closed the door.

August 1960
(later set to music)

**And the angel of the LORD
went further, and stood
in a narrow place,
where was no way to turn
either to the right hand
or to the left.**
Numbers 22:26

With Tears in My Heart—the Poems of Gertrude Grace Sanborn

I'll Build a Fence Around Today

I'll build a fence around today;
Within its limits, I will stay.
Therein I walk my path alone
With none to share or little own.

Within these walls is wondrous peace;
And, tho confined, I find release.
For God's own Son doth walk with me
To comfort and give liberty.

I'll look not thru its sheltering bar,
Nor let tomorrow's problems mar
The peace I have within this wall
Because my Lord arranged it all.

Enough for me to live today
And be content herein to stay
Till God's dear Son doth op' the door
To leave today forevermore.

1960
set to music by the author

Folio X—God's Will

Captive Am I

Captive am I
In a body
Which limits
My heart's pure desire,
Held in its bondage
An earthling
While my spirit
Great heights
Doth aspire.

About 1959

I find then a law, that,
when I would do good, evil is present with me.
For I delight in the law of God after the inward man:
But I see another law in my members,
warring against the law of my mind,
and bringing me into captivity to the law of sin which is in my members.
O wretched man that I am! who shall deliver me from the body of this
death? I thank God through Jesus Christ our Lord.
So then with the mind I myself serve the law of God;
but with the flesh the law of sin.

Romans 7:21 - 8:1

Life

Yesterday: but a doorway
Into the hall of life;
Today: a little platform
Where we may rest from strife;
Tomorrow: the journey's end
When all our dreams come true;
Together: but the span of life
We all must needs pass thru.

April 1958

What *is* your life?
It is even a vapour,
that appeareth
for a little time,
and then
vanisheth
away.
James 4:14

Folio X—God's Will

Far Better for Me

I was trusting my Lord
Until somebody said,
"How can you bear that load?"
I had pressed right on
With heart held high
Until I felt that goad.

Then self-pity engulfed me,
And rebellion began;
And it seemed too hard was my race;
So I wept in despair and started to cry
And took my eyes from His face.

Now I know they mean well
And perhaps love me more
Who wonder because of my trial;
But far better for me
If I have no one to care
Than to not see His face for a while.

October 1957
Atlanta, Georgia

For Jesus

Washing, ironing, making beds;
Cooking, cleaning, baking breads;
Always busy without pay,
I'll do it all for Jesus.

He's coming back one busy day
As I work and while I pray;
He'll bring a crown for faithfulness;
So, I'll do my work for Jesus.

Tho I labor hard and long,
I'll be glad and sing this song;
For at His coming I shall know
How I do it all for Jesus.

1945

> Whether therefore ye eat,
> or drink
> or whatsoever ye do,
> do all to the glory of God.
> *1 Corinthians 10:31*

Folio X—God's Will

The Singing Heart

I opened my eyes this morning;
My heart began to sing
A new day to give to Jesus
A new day to live for Him.

His mercies are new each morning,
His blessings every day.
New strength and new faith He gives me
To walk thru a bright new day.

Our God who is rich in mercy
Who grants me the grace each day
To wake from my sleep each morning
His precepts to keep each day.

Amazing that I, a creature
Made by His mighty hand,
May live each new day for Jesus
Till I in His presence stand.

Thru night hours he keeps me safely
My cares on Him I lay;
With dawn comes a day to serve Him
A new day to walk His way.

He knows of each passing hour
And what is there within;
He gives me there time and privilege
A new day to live for Him.

If I Could Paint a Lovely Picture

If I could paint a lovely picture
That would show the joy that's in my soul,
I'd sit before an easel
And paint until I reached my goal.

If I could sing a song like angels,
I'd climb the highest hill and sing.
I'd swell the music forth forever
For the theme of song is my King.

If I could write a book as great men,
I'd write with ink of purest gold.
I'd underline the word Redeemer;
I'd write till everything was told.

If I could give a great oration
And move my audience to tears,
I'd stand upon my feet and gesture
And keep on speaking thru the years.

But I am but a simple person;
I cannot paint, nor write, nor sing;
So, I'll bow my heart, and pray, and praise Him.
Thus to Christ my witness bring.

1946

Folio X—God's Will

One Day at a Time

One day at a time
With its gold or its dross;
One day at a time
With its profit or loss;
One day at a time
With its joy or its tear;
One day at a time
With its faith or its fear;
Just one day
One day at a time.

September 1963

**Take therefore no thought for the morrow:
for the morrow shall take thought for the things of itself.
Sufficient unto the day *is* the evil thereof.**
Matthew 6:34

Folio XI

Death

O death, where *is* thy sting?
O grave, where *is* thy victory?
The sting of death *is* sin;
and the strength of sin *is* the law.
But thanks *be* to God,
which giveth us the victory
through our Lord Jesus Christ.
1 Corinthians 15:55-57

With Tears in My Heart—the Poems of Gertrude Grace Sanborn

Which One?

Who decides which one should go?
Who is wise enough to know?
Should I, in death, precede my love?
Should he leave me for realms above?

Only God the choice can make.
Which one to leave, which one to take.
But this I know, and His will I own--
To take away or leave alone.

📖

**Precious
in the sight of the LORD
is the death
of his saints.**
Psalm 116:15

Folio XI--Death

More Than Mary

"They have taken away my Lord!"
She wept, for He was not there.
She did not believe He was risen
And so was in deep despair!

But we understand more than Mary,
For God had raised His Dear Son.
So let us not weep in the garden
At the grave of our dear absent one.

April 1955

And they say unto her,
Woman, why weepest thou?
She saith unto them,
Because they have taken away Lord,
and I know not where they have laid him.
John 20:13

Night Watch

I sat and watched
While pain racked and tore my dear one;
I watched in tears
As I beheld his awful powers.
I prayed to God
To overthrow that demon;
I sat and watched
Thru lonely night-time hours.

I stood and saw
That cruel monster hurt her;
I was so weak
Beside his wicked powers.
It broke my heart
To see her bruised and broken;
I stood my watch
Thru lonely night time hours.

I waited there
To see if I could comfort;
My arms of love
I offered tenderly.
I spent myself
And all my human powers;
And there was I
Thru lonely night time hours.

October 12, 1952 (At the hospital with Audrey)
In her own handwriting at the bottom of this poem, the author penned "Pain personified!" Audrey, Gertrude's second born, died the end of November 1952.

Folio XI--Death

Sunrise & Morning Star

The poet writes a sad, sad song
Of sunset and the dark;
Of evening star and parting
While loathing to embark.

I write of tender longings
And wait the while I write,
For sweet will be the meeting
When faith gives way to sight.

Sunrise and morning star
And one clear, clear call for me;
And may there be sweet singing at the bar
When I put out to sea.

Day dawn and trumpet sound
And after that the Light;
And there will be no sadness there
When faith give way to sight.

For tho I've been a stranger here
And cares beset me sore,
I know I'll see Him face to face
When I have crossed the bar.

About 1942

With Tears in My Heart—the Poems of Gertrude Grace Sanborn

Death Came in the Room

Death came in the room that dark morning
And sat at the head of her bed.
He chilled the dear form of our sick one;
And then, interrupted, he fled.

But Death is tenacious and certain;
He returned when we thought him not near.
He cruelly laid hold of our darling
And left her asleep on her bier.

November 30, 1952
Daughter Audrey died on a Sunday afternoon at Berea Hospital in Berea, Ohio.
Her father and Mel were there. The author regretfully wrote, "I was home."
She had just gone home to rest. Audrey was twenty years old.

Folio XI--Death

Resurrection

I planted a bulb in the fall of the year,
Expecting a bloom in the spring,
And covered it o'er with the spadefuls of earth;
It was just an ugly brown thing.

The winter snows came and the rain and the sun;
And a flower rose up from the dead
With beautiful fragrance and wonderful bloom--
Just as the gardener had said.

I've laid my beloved away in the grave,
Expecting to see her some day;
They've covered her o'er with the spadefuls of earth;
It was just her frail body of clay.

Life's chill days will come
Till the voice of God's Son
Calls my dear one to wake from the dead--
Just as the Scripture has said.

April 1953
To my daughter Audrey whom we laid away December 3, 1952

Stay Thy Hand

Stay thy hand, O Time,
And do not touch my mother;
Keep back thy fingers
From her dear, sweet face;
Wait thou with brush of grey
And weight for stooping;
Hold back thy hand
And show her only grace.
Stay thy hand, O Time,
And do thy work to others;
Tread slowly, Time,
And over-look my mother;
Yea, sleep awhile,
And be slow to wake again.

July 8, 1943
Written on the author's mother's birthday

Folio XI--Death

Safe in Christ

Into Christ's glorious presence
Close by His pure pierced side,
Ever beholding His beauty
Our dear one has gone to abide.

Listens to songs of the angels,
Leans her dear head on His breast,
There gently we leave our beloved
Knowing how greatly she's blessed.

Tho we have grief since she's left us,
Still we have peace at the thought
That she is safe in His presence;
For her, all life's battles are fought.

Compare Job 38:7 where "the morning stars [angels] *sang together."*

📖

**For I am persuaded,
that neither death, nor life,
nor angels, nor principalities, nor powers,
nor things present, nor things to come,
Nor height, nor depth, nor any other creature,
shall be able to separate us from the love of God,
which is in Christ Jesus our Lord.**
Romans 8:38-39

What Will I Say?

If God should call for me
Before I spend this day
If He should summon me
While going on my way
If He should stop the plans
Which I have carefully laid
If He should call me Home
Before they're even made.

If God should call for me
While busy at my task
If He should stop my steps
Before I speak or ask
If He should take my breath
My heart's poor feeble beat
If He should call today
Would I His favor meet?

If God should call for me
While I'm asleep at night
If He should move me up
From darkness into light
If He should call me now
And leave a vacant place
If He should take me home
Could I His judgment face?

Folio XI--Death

Chorus:
What will I say when I see Him?
What will I say when He calls?
What will I say to my Saviour
Who willingly gave me His all?
What will I say when I see Him?
What will I say to my God?
If I know I have given the most of my life
To the things of this earth
I have trod?

1964 Set to music

With Tears in My Heart—the Poems of Gertrude Grace Sanborn

The Key to Tomorrow

I have peered and have guessed;
I have planned and have pressed;
But God held the key to Tomorrow.

I have wished I had died;
I have fretted and cried;
But naught has He shown of Tomorrow.

I have hardened my heart
And have wanted no part
In the vale which we call Tomorrow.

But though God in His grace
Has not shown me my place,
He has written His Word for Tomorrow.

And there in the Unknown
Sitteth Love on His throne,
And He has The Plan for Tomorrow.

November, 1952,
Written to Audrey's sweetheart who could not bear "Tomorrow" without her.
He was married later to a lovely woman who made him happy--and this is how
it should be.

Folio XI--Death

Ours For a Moment

Loaned to our arms for a moment,
Left in our care for a day;
Entrusted were we with a treasure
Until she was taken away.

We scarcely had time but to name her;
Yet it seems she's been ours from the start.
Amazing how we grew to love her;
So great was her hold on our heart.

But now on our kind Father's bosom,
Enclosed in His great arms of love,
Lies our precious and beautiful baby,
Who has left us for living above.

Yet better are we for the moment;
For since she's been taken away,
Our hearts are now drawn to that Glory,
Where we know we shall see her someday.

February 1974
Written to her assistant pastor when he and his wife
lost their one-month-old baby girl.

Folio XII

Heaven

And God shall wipe away
all tears from their eyes;
and there shall be no more death,
neither sorrow, nor crying,
neither shall there be
any more pain:
for the former things
are passed away.
Revelation 21:4

With Tears in My Heart—the Poems of Gertrude Grace Sanborn

In My Father's House

In my Father's House are many mansions;
There someday with Him I will reside.
When my journey's o'er and life has ended,
In my Father's House I will abide.

When my heart is troubled with its burdens
And the things of earth grow very dim,
I just turn my heart and think of Heaven,
To my Father's House and yearn for Him.

In my Father's House I'll see my dear ones,
And I'll meet the patriarchs of old;
I will praise His name that He has gone there
To provide for me that blest abode.

O my heart is stirred when e'er I read it
That He'll come and call my name one day
And take me up to meet Him in the Glory
To my Father's House, and there to stay.

September 1981

Folio XII--Heaven

At Home with Him

At home with Him and willing rather
To leave this house of clay and earthly care
To dwell with Him, by His dear side be present--
Should I not joy to think I soon may share

That place above, eternal in the Heavens,
Prepared of God to make my rest complete;
To be with Christ, to see and hear Him speaking,
To spend my days just living at His feet?

At home, at peace, at rest--I love the prospect.
Tho dear ones here and friends are good and true.
My home in Heaven allures me, and I wait
To hear the Trump or walk the Valley thru.

1944
This poem was read by Pastor Earl Willetts at Audrey Sanborn's funeral. Audrey was Gertrude's and Ren's second-born daughter who went Home to be with the Lord at age twenty after a valiant fight with Hodgkin's disease.

In my Father's house are many mansions:
if *it were* not *so,* I would have told you.
I go to prepare a place for you.
And if I go and prepare a place for you,
I will come again, and receive you unto myself;
that where I am, *there* ye may be also.
John 14:2-3

She's Gone!

The sparkle has gone from our family;
The glitter has gone from our name.
The purpose has gone for our meetings,
And nothing is just quite the same.

So proud was she of her family;
Her sons were her joy and her crown;
To her they were men of great honor
And merchants of wealth and renown.

Tho she was unlearned, she was clever
In getting her way and her wish;
And was ever so skilled in her kitchen
To make up a wonderful dish.

Thru years of much testing and trial,
She never did whimper nor cry;
But came thru it all like a soldier
And ever her grey head held high.

When sad she would never admit it;
When weary she never would rest;
She strove every way to be better;
And then, to be better, than best.

Folio XII--Heaven

One day from His Counsels of Heaven
God called her dear name from the sky;
And she left us--so quickly she left us;
She left us without a "good bye."

Yes, the sparkle has gone from our family,
And the light of our clan has grown dim;
For our vivacious and dear little Mother
Has gone up to Heaven with Him.

January 1962
The author was Florence Van Tassel Sanborn's daughter-in-law. She wrote of her Mother-in-law, "Mother died November 30, 1960 at the age of eighty-four. She was a remarkable woman." They had a very special relationship.

As the Days Move On

As the days move on
And I leave the past behind,
Much I thought was wisdom
So foolish now I find.
And hours I thought so trying
Seem now as passing free;
And in the light of Heaven
How puny shown to be.
All those years
Now do not matter;
His plan was best for me.

1960
set to music

Folio XII--Heaven

Since I've Seen His Face

I have seen the face of Jesus
With his beauty fair and pure;
I have glimpsed His perfect glory
And this world has lost its lure;
I have had a glimpse of heaven,
And its wondrous sounds I hear;
I have known His peace and promise,
And I know I need no fear.

I have read the Holy Scriptures,
And my heart I guided right;
I have read His plan and purpose,
And my soul has seen the light;
I have heard His sweet voice calling
As He clearly spoke my name;
He has called me to his service;
In surrender full I came.

Refrain:
I'm not the same
Since I met Jesus;
My life has changed
Since I've known His grace;
The things of earth
Have lost their glamour
Since I have seen His lovely face.

Words set to music

Only a Moment

Only a moment
Then hours forever;
Just for today
Then years by His side;
Suffering awhile
Then called into Glory;
Now for a season
Then to abide.

Here light affliction
But there weight of glory;
Manifold trials
There found to His praise.
Songs in the night here
But there only morning;
Here but the earnest
There always day.

Now we are tenting
In Heaven a mansion;
This clay to crumble
There gold to stand;
Sands always shifting
The Rock firm forever;
Wilderness waiting
There reward from His hand.

Folio XII--Heaven

Only a moment
Tho it may seem long;
Now for a season
We sing faith's glad song.
Only a moment
To run life's short race;
Only a moment
'Till we see His face.

1943; (set to music by the author)

For our light affliction, which is but for a moment,
worketh for us a far more exceeding *and* eternal weight of glory;
While we look not at the things which are seen,
but at the things which are not seen:
for the things which are seen *are* temporal;
but the things which are not seen *are* eternal.
2 Corinthians 4:17-18

Now for a season . . . ye are in heaviness through manifold temptations:
That the trial of your faith . . . might be found unto praise and honour and
glory at the appearing of Jesus Christ:
1 Peter 1:6-7

Folio XIII

The Holy Spirit

But the Comforter, *which is* the Holy Ghost,
whom the Father will send in my name,
he shall teach you all things,
and bring all things to your remembrance,
whatsoever I have said unto you.
John 14:26

In the Spirit

Tho my feet are in stocks
From this world's weight and care,
My hands, too, are shackled and bound.
Tho my body's imprisoned,
My lips covered o'er,
My stopped ears cannot hear a sound.

I can look far away
From these fetters of clay,
And I find I can hear; I can see;
I can sing in my heart;
I can mount up with wings,
For God's Spirit
Is dwelling in me.

Folio XIII—The Holy Spirit

To the Spirit

Spirit of Light, illumine me;
Light all my vision with love;
Show me the Lord in His righteousness;
Show me His glories above.

Spirit of Truth, sweep over me;
Teach me and lead me to pray;
Open my lips and encourage me,
Telling me just what to say.

Spirit of Christ, live out thru me
Jesus the pure Holy One.
Manifest Him so others may see
The grace which in me is done.

Spirit of God, Thy presence Divine
Dwelling in temples of clay
Changing and keeping and pledging to me
That I shall be like Him someday.

1946

And whatsoever ye shall ask in my name, that will I do,
that the Father may be glorified in the Son.
John 14:13

Praise to the Holy Spirit

Holy Spirit, Christians' Guide,
Walking ever by my side
Leading me in paths of Grace
Showing me His lovely face.

Holy Spirit, earnest Friend,
Constant Helper to the end
Urging me to put away
Things of pride, and things of clay.

Holy One, sent in His name
From the Father's Glory came;
Came to dwell and to abide,
Live in my heart, stay by my side.

Holy One of Truth and Light,
Glowing in this realm of night;
Here because Christ went away,
Staying till He comes some day.

Holy One, who made me cry,
"ABBA," to my Father in the sky;
Intercessor in each prayer,
Gift of God, Thy work my care.

1944

Folio XIII—The Holy Spirit

Stop Awhile

When the Holy Spirit speaks to me
Saying stop awhile and pray,
Many times I say "TOO BUSY,"
And I go along my way.

That day is full of trials,
And the labor seems so long;
The cares of it oppress me,
And I find I have no song.

BUT--When the Holy Spirit speaks to me
And I stop my course and pray
And heed His voice so tender,
I kneel down to God and say:

"Thank You, Lord, for calling me!
I am so bent to sin,
And I know I'd soon forget to pray
But for Him who dwells within."

And so I pray, and praise, and learn
Sweet lessons at His feet;
I find it's there I get the strength
The daily tasks to meet!

1937

Folio XIV

Prayer

Be careful for nothing; but in every thing
by prayer and supplication with thanksgiving
let your requests be made known unto God.
And the peace of God, which passeth all understanding,
shall keep your hearts and minds through Christ Jesus.
Philippians 4:6-7

I Long Ago Decided

I long ago decided
Tho oft' it's hard to bear
My Lord in love doth try me
To keep my heart at prayer.

Tho I do weep and mourn it
As He lays His hand on me,
My Lord doth know I'd wander
So He's restricted me.

It seems so very trying
And often most unfair,
Yet always doth He love me
And show His tender care.

Thru days which test and try me,
I'll trust His better way.
I know He knows the lessons
I need from day to day.

1959

Folio XIV--Prayer

I Can Tell Thee, Lord

I am so glad, dear Lord, to say
That one day long ago
I learned to pray and tell to Thee
My every care and woe.

For since I am a mother
And now so long a wife,
How many strange and oft' hard things
Do come into my life.

I cannot tell these secret cares
To other ears but Thine.
They either sound too dreadful
Or I appear to whine.

I would not cast aspersion
On those I hold so dear;
Yet they do cause me problems
Perplexity and fear.

So many things I do not know;
Seems much I'll never learn;
I could not tell another;
They would not e'en discern.

But Thou, dear Lord, my friend so true
Who formed my frail, weak frame,
I'm glad I can confide in you
And Thine attention claim.

September 1961

The Name of the Lord

The name of the Lord is a Strong Tower;
The Righteous run there and are safe;
The name of the Lord is my Refuge,
The place I may hide and escape.
The name of the Lord is a Strong Tower;
Therein I find comfort and grace
To rest from my day
To read and to pray.
The name of the Lord is my Tower.

1963
(set to music by the author)

**The name of the LORD *is* a strong tower:
the righteous runneth into it, and is safe.**
Proverbs 18:10

Folio XIV--Prayer

Lord, Give Me a Tender Heart

Lord, give me a tender heart
Moved to love the weary.
Teach me, O Lord,
Just what to say
To burdened ones and dreary.

Lord, give me a loving heart
With eyes to see their need.
Teach me, O Lord,
Just how to pray
And for their case to plead.

Lord, give me a weeping heart
To weep with those who cry.
Teach me, O Lord,
To comfort them
And not to pass them by.

Lord, give me a heart like Thine
Tender and loving and true.
Teach me, my Lord, Thy tenderness;
Teach me this work to do.

1964

I Thank Thee, Lord

I thank Thee, Lord, for Thy grace
That draws me close in life's strange race.

I trust Thee, Lord, for each new day
So I may walk anew Thy way.

I tell Thee, Lord, of each hard night--
Its wakeful hours, its tears and fright.

I wait, dear Lord, and rest in Thee;
For at the End, Thy face I'll see.

I press toward the mark for the prize
of the high calling of God in Christ Jesus.
Philippians 3:14

Folio XIV--Prayer

Intercession

The Father knows your heartache;
He hears your faintest cry;
And all the while you're anxious,
He's guarding with His eye.

The Spirit knows your problem;
He whispers in my ear:
"A saint is sad and crying,
Is overcome by fear."

I raise my heart to Heaven;
I tell Father there
That one He loves is anxious
And needs His loving care.

Then the loving Saviour
Takes my humble plea
And places it with your prayer
Which has preceded me.

Then He sends His warm compassion
And sweet peace upon your soul
As you learn to lean on Jesus
And to let Him take control.

1945

I Bring My Heart to Thee

Dear Lord, I bring my heart to Thee;
Renew its feeble beat;
For, Lord, I come dependently
For strength my task to meet.
I bring my lips to Thee today;
O frame them to Thy praise;
Lead my song as I walk along
Thru life's dim misty haze.

Dear Lord, I bring my will to Thee;
O bend it to Thy way;
O Lord, I come expectantly
For grace and help today.
I bring myself to Thee, dear Lord;
O use my all I pray
And fill my heart with words of love
To drop along life's way.

Dear Lord, I bring my mind to Thee;
Renew its little thought;
For, Lord, I come submissively,
Am seeking to be taught.
I bring my plans to Thee, dear Lord,
And place them at Thy feet;
O teach me, Lord, Thy Holy Truth
In all its beauty sweet.

October, 1964

Folio XIV--Prayer

My Morning Prayer

Dear Lord,
I raise my heart in praise
As morning gives its early rays
And thank Thee for a fresh new day
To live for Thee and walk Thy way.

Dear Lord,
I magnify Thy name,
For Thou art ever more the same;
And thank Thee for Thy Word so true
With every promise proven thru.

Dear Lord,
I thank Thee for my morning meal
And for the strength and health I feel;
I thank Thee, too, for home and mate,
Protective care and my estate.

Dear Lord,
What grace that such as I
May speak my heart to One so High,
And tell in word of human phrase
My heart's own thanks and deepest praise.

August 1961

Morning Prayer

Each day I turn my heart to Thee
And bring my morning prayer;
I tell Thee all my problems
And cast on Thee my care.

I cannot heal the heartache
Or others' burdens bear,
But I know God can and will
Solve all their grief and care.

Through all my nights you've kept me
While I sleep unmindfully
Of Thy great power and wisdom
That watches over me.

1981

Folio XIV--Prayer

Praise to Jesus

O Jesus, I love Thee
Because Thou art fair
Because of Thy beauty
Which none can compare.

O Master, I love Thee
Because Thou art strong
Because of Thy power
I'm kept all along.

O Saviour, I love Thee
Because Thou didst die
Because Thou hast saved me
Tho sinful am I.

O blessed and Holy and wonderful Lord,
O precious and cleansing Inspiring Word,
I praise Thee and hail Thee,
Thou blest Three in One;
I long to be with Thee
When this life is done.

1940

Forgive My Heart

I know the coldness of my heart;
I know how far I've gone astray;
I've let the cares of life come in
And draw my tired heart away.
O draw me back and hold me close;
And turn me back unto Thy way.
Revive my heart; renew my faith today!

I grow so weary in the race;
I grow so tired in the fray.
I've let the things of life come in
And take my joy and peace away.
O draw me back and hold me close;
And turn me back unto Thy way.
Revive my heart; renew my faith today.

Coda:
Revive my heart;
Refresh my life;
Renew my faith I pray.
Revive my heart;
Refresh my life today.
O turn me back
And lift me up;
And hold me close, dear Lord.
Revive my heart;
Refresh my life;
Renew my faith I pray.

December 1964

Folio XIV--Prayer

Cries My Heart to Thee Today

Show me, Lord, Thy loving hand
The path where I should go;
Show me, Father, as I cry
From hurt and cruel blow!

Show me--I do not see with eyes my own.
Lead me, Lord; I am weak, tired, and alone;
Hold my hand, Thou One so Mighty;
Cries my heart to Thee, O God!

All my ways seem bare and friendless--
Every well I have filled up with earth;
Disappointment stills my song,
Too stunned am I for joy and mirth!

Clear away, my God, the barriers and the mountains
That loom before me bleak and cold and gray;
Use me, Lord, to show to all Thy praises;
Help me now the more to trust and pray!

Hold me close, Thou One so Mighty,
Cries my heart to Thee today!

1944

Sup with Me

Enter in, Thou Blessed Knocker;
Sup with me--just You and I;
I will feast on food so filling;
Sup with me; don't pass me by.

Sit with me beside still waters
Where the lovely pastures grow;
Feed my soul on Thine own self, Lord;
Teach me there Thy will to know.

Enter in, Thou Blessed Knocker;
How can I refuse this grace?
Just to think the Lord of Glory
Will come in, speak face to face.

Sup with me, Thou Blessed Knocker;
How I long to lay my head
On Thy bosom, close communion;
Sup with me, Thou Living Bread.

1943

Behold, I stand at the door, and knock:
if any man hear my voice, and open the door,
I will come in to him, and will sup with him, and he with me.
Revelation 3:20

Folio XIV--Prayer

Show Me Jesus as I Read

Take this eager heart
And this poor, dull mind;
Show me in Thy Word
The treasures I may find.

Thou hast made me, God;
Thou knowest well my frame.
O waft from Page to being
The perfume of Christ's name.

Take these ears so stopped,
And let them hear Thy voice
Calling me to worship Him
And in His love rejoice.

Take these eyes so blind
And make them keen to see
Jesus Christ, the lovely One,
There on the Page for me.

1943

**Open thou mine eyes,
that I may behold wondrous things
out of thy law.**
Psalm 119:18

Thank You, Lord

We thank you, Lord,
For our food
And that our needs
Are understood.

We thank Thee, Lord,
For strength and life
For wit to battle
Work and strife.

We thank Thee, Lord,
For children dear;
We pray that we
May keep them near.

We thank Thee, Lord,
For our home
And pray there'll be
No cause to roam.

We thank Thee, Lord,
For family care,
For joy it brings
Beyond compare.

Folio XIV--Prayer

We thank Thee, Lord,
For God in Thee
For promise of
Eternity.

For mansions bright
Where we shall meet
And sit before
Thy Holy feet.

This a prayer
From grateful heart,
But thanking Thee
'Tis but a start.

1936
Probably the second poem the author ever composed.

Teach Me, O Lord!

Teach me Thy Word, O Lord,
That I may see Thy face,
That I may grow in grace,
That I may run life's race;
Teach me Thy word.

Teach me Thy word, O Lord,
That I may teach another,
That I may love my brother,
And be a better mother;
Teach me Thy Word.

Teach me Thy Word, O Lord,
That I may trust each day,
That I may truly pray,
That I the Truth obey;
Teach me Thy Word.

August 1963

So then faith cometh by hearing, and hearing by the word of God.
Romans 1:17

Folio XIV--Prayer

I Love Thee, Lord

I love Thee, Lord,
For taking me,
An outcast stained by sin,
And calling me in wondrous grace
And letting me come in.

To think that I
Of Adam's race
Am now a child of Thine
Just bows my heart
And melts my will;
I would be wholly Thine.

1957

But God, who is rich in mercy,
for his great love wherewith he loved us,
Even when we were dead in sins,
hath quickened us together with Christ,
(by grace ye are saved;)
And hath raised *us* up together,
and made *us* sit together
in heavenly *places* in Christ Jesus:
Ephesians 2:4-6

We Pray Thy Blessing, Lord

We pray Thy blessing, Lord,
As we before Thee bow;
Please look upon us from above
And touch our hearts just now.

We pray Thy blessing, Lord,
And sing our hymns of praise;
Draw nigh to us, dear Saviour,
And dwell there all our days.

1946

Folio XIV--Prayer

A Prayer

When the promptings of the Spirit say
It's time to kneel and pray,
I find a quiet corner
And look up to God and say:

"O Lord of all creation,
I praise Thy Holy name
And marvel at Thy kindness
Which is every day the same."

"That Thou who didst make Heaven,
The sun and stars to shine,
Have considered me in all my sin
And sent Thy Son divine."

O, teach me how to witness
To Thy love and care for me
That by Thy Holy Spirit
I may lead some soul to Thee.

Thank you for Thy Word, dear Lord,
So that I can plainly see
The great and precious promises
That Thou hast offered me. Amen.

1939 LaGrange, Ohio

With Tears in My Heart—the Poems of Gertrude Grace Sanborn

Are You Tired and Weary?

Are you tired and weary?
Does your day seem long?
Is your burden heavy?
Has your heart no song?

Then start the day by praying;
God will lighten every care
As you bow your knee in reverence,
And lift up your heart in prayer.

1943

Humble yourselves therefore
under the mighty hand of God,
that he may exalt you in due time:
Casting all your care upon him;
for he careth for you.
1 Peter 5:6-7

Cast thy burden upon the LORD,
and he shall sustain thee:
he shall never suffer the righteous to be moved.
Psalm 55:22

Folio XIV--Prayer

A Mother's Prayer

O Lord, I want to be a mother
Who will carry out Thy will
And do all things to please Thee
As I all my duties fill.

O Lord, I want to be a mother
Who will show her children God,
Who will point them to the Saviour
Who once this cold world trod.

O Lord, I want to be a mother
Who will witness to Thy love,
Who will show by word and action
That her strength is from above.

O Lord, I want to be a mother
Who will do a work for Thee,
And who will be a good example
To the ones you've given me.

October 1943

With Tears in My Heart—the Poems of Gertrude Grace Sanborn

Be Still My Soul

O then be still, my soul.
Why art thou now cast down?
Put thou thy trust in God
Who has for thee a crown.
O lift thine heart, my soul,
For God is on His throne;
And hope in God, my soul,
Who careth for His own.
O then be still, my soul.

1961
a song

Why art thou cast down, O my soul?
and *why* art thou disquieted in me?
hope thou in God:
for I shall yet praise him
for the help of his countenance.
Psalm 42:5

Folio XIV--Prayer

I Have Not Talked to Thee

O Lord, I have not talked to Thee today
Nor thanked Thee for this life to live for Thee.
The cares have pressed and nearly overwhelmed me;
And yet, O Lord, I have not talked to Thee.

It seems to me too much I have to bear,
Too great the load of care I have from Thee;
Still in my weakness, Lord, I have not
Bowed my heart and turned to talk to Thee.

So teach me now that I may not grow weary
Because of things which in Thy plan allow;
Draw me to pray, to come to Thee expectant
For all I need--for every need--just now.

1955 Montreal

With Tears in My Heart—the Poems of Gertrude Grace Sanborn

I Thank Thee, Lord

Dear Lord, I raise my heart in praise
As morning gives its early rays,
And thank Thee for a clean new day
To live for Thee and walk Thy way.
And, Lord, I magnify Thy name
For Thou art evermore the same,
And thank Thee for Thy Word so true,
And every promise proven thru
Which is in the very mind of You.
I thank Thee for my morning meal
And for the strength and health I feel;
I thank Thee, too, for home and mate,
Protective care that compensates.
O Lord, what grace that I may speak
To Thee my God--my day's complete,
That I may tell in words so plain
My hearts own praise, I will proclaim!

One of the author's latter poems found after death in her own hand writing. Gertrude Sanborn died in June of 1988. This was probably written a year or more before her death.

Folio XIV--Prayer

Lord, Help Me to Pray

Lord, call me to pray.
I am so weary I can scarcely speak;
My mind is tired and I am weak.
Lord, draw me to pray.
I need Thy strength and help this hour;
I need to hear Thy voice of cheer and love and power.
Lord, help me to pray.
I fear lest I cannot call out to Thee;
I hide my sick self away in misery,
And I forget how to pray.

1984

Come unto me, all *ye* that labour
and are heavy laden,
and I will give you rest.
Take my yoke upon you,
and learn of me;
for I am meek and lowly in heart:
and ye shall find rest unto your souls.
For my yoke *is* easy,
and my burden is light.
Matthew 11:28-30

With Tears in My Heart—the Poems of Gertrude Grace Sanborn

Lead Me to the Rock

Lead me to the Rock
That is higher than I.
Lead me to the Rock;
Lord, attend unto my cry.
When my heart is overwhelmed
And my spirit wonders, "Why?"
Lead me to the Rock
That is higher than I.

July 1961
Set to music

Hear my cry, O God; attend unto my prayer.
From the end of the earth will I cry unto thee,
when my heart is overwhelmed:
Lead me to the rock *that* is higher than I.
For thou hast been a shelter for me,
and a strong tower from the enemy.
Psalm 61:1-3

Folio XIV--Prayer

Lord, I Have a Burden

Dear Lord, I have a burden
That none may know but Thee.
I come to Thee, my Father,
In quiet secrecy.

I cannot solve this problem,
I cannot meet the need;
And so I come to Thee, Oh Lord,
And for Thy wisdom plead.

I may not tell another
Or any part disclose;
Yet, Lord, I know you understand;
For Thou my burden knows.

July 1961

Cast thy burden upon the LORD,
and he shall sustain thee:
he shall never suffer the righteous to be moved.
Psalm 55:22

More Than These

How much do I love Thee, Lord Jesus?
How deep is my love for Thee?
Is it more than for fairest of treasures?
Is it more than for beauty of sea?

Is it more than for sun's morning splendor?
Is it more than for evening's warm glow?
Is it more than for beautiful flowers?
Or the beauty of glistening snow?

Do I love Thee more than my children?
More than my friends or my mate?
Do I love Thee more than my silver,
Or more, than my house or estate?

"Lovest thou me?" He has challenged;
So deep is His question I wait
And probe in my heart the true answer;
And I find that I oft' hesitate.

How much do I love Thee, Lord Jesus?
I bow my poor heart as I say,
"I love Thee, yea Lord, I do love Thee;
But I would love Thee more every day."

John 21:15
1981

Folio XIV--Prayer

My Times Are in Thy Hands

Such hands as Thine
Can never fail nor falter;
My times, my goings, and my comings
Thou dost know.
So strong--such hands,
So wise in all their moving,
Directing worlds and all the teeming
Nations here below!

Thy hands, my God,
Are holding me!
My times so small they seem
As I compare
Thy hands which wrote the Law
And shook the Mountain.
Those hands deal tenderly with me in care!

My times, Thy hands!
Sweet peace I find in this, O Lord,
And grace to meet the problems of each day.
So I put my hand in Thine,
O God my Father;
And holding thus will walk my brief
And earthly way!

Psalms 31:15
October 1949
during a period of illness

Such Things I Have to Tell Thee

Such things I have to tell thee, Lord,
    Of praise and answered prayer,
    Of overcoming faith and grace,
        Of all Thy faithful care.

Such things I have to tell Thee, Lord,
    Of songs within my heart,
    Of words of peace and comfort
        Which each day newly start.

Such things I have to tell Thee, Lord,
    Of longings and desire,
    Of yearning expectations,
        And dreams which did expire.

Such things I have to tell Thee, Lord,
    Of all my life's long way--
Of pain and hurt and sleepless nights,
        And waitings every day.

Such things I have to tell Thee, Lord;
    My heart is brimming full
    Of cares and disappointments,
        And things quite pitiful.

Folio XIV--Prayer

I claim thine ear to understand;
I know you'll heed my call
Of each and everything I say;
I know you'll hear it all.

Dear Lord, just keep my heart in touch;
And make me so in tune
That I can tell such things to Thee,
And wait Thy coming soon.

January 1963

O Jesus

O Jesus, gives me patience
As I struggle thru each day;
O Saviour, help me conquer
The forces in my way.

The things, dear Lord, that hinder
My growth and usefulness--
That make me tired and weary
And filled with hopelessness.

O help me to surrender
To Thy Holy Spirit, Lord,
And teach me that this chastening
Will be fruitful afterward.

O put thine arms around me
And shelter with Thy love--
Thou blessed intercessor,
Thou Son of God above.

1939

Folio XIV--Prayer

Pathway of This Day

Within Thy purposes, O Lord,
Is kept the pathway of this day.
Thy hand unrolls each little moment
As I walk along its way.

Tho I step into some sorrow,
Thou hast known it all along;
Should I find my pace to falter,
Thou art near with arm so strong.

If I meet distress or problem,
I'll not stumble in dismay;
For Thy purpose is accomplished
While I walk along this day.

July 1965

With Tears in My Heart—the Poems of Gertrude Grace Sanborn

What Is It, Lord?

What is it you want from me, dear Lord?
You are dealing so sternly these days.
What should I do or leave undone,
Or how shall I change my ways?

What is it you want from me, dear Lord?
Is it worship or work or means?
Show me Thy will, and help me to learn
What it is that you want from me!

1980

Folio XIV--Prayer

Above the Din

Above the din and noise and strife,
Above the cares of my own life;
O Lord, I come to Thee and pray;
Now teach me, Lord, just what to say.

For self I cry, "I need Thy touch!"
For I do murmur ever much;
For others dear I yearn and plead
That Thou wilt grant their every need.

My Lord, I long to come to Thee
So free and oft that I may be
In reverent attitude all day
To lift my heart and learn to pray.

August 1961

**And the work of righteousness shall be peace;
and the effect of righteousness
quietness and assurance for ever.**
Isaiah 32:17

A Prayer for Trust

Help me to trust Thee
For all of my days;
Teach me, O Father,
To rest in Thy ways.
Thou who hast formed me
And planned all my years
Art greater than trials,
Disappointments, and tears.

1951

Thy Face

Lord, let me see Thy precious face;
'Twill draw me on in this hard race.
Nothing lovely here I see
Save pain and tears and misery.
O show to me in tender grace
The light of Glory in Thy face.
Illumine me in this dark night,
And let my heart behold this sight.

March 1953

Folio XIV--Prayer

Lord of My Years

My years--all Thine, O Lord--
I would not change them if I could.
Thy way was best though not always understood.
The years have mounted; the path is often steep.
Yet, on the rocky places, Thou my feet doth keep.

The light ahead grows brighter and more clear.
Thy Word of promise becomes more precious & so dear.
And into Thy hands I commit my treasure dear--
My feeble child, my helpless Beverly.

*The author was concerned for her retarded
daughter after the author would die.*

At Night I Lie in Bed and Think of Thee

At night I lie in bed and think of Thee, O Lord,
Of how my life is in Thy hands and purpose.
I think of all the cares and mysteries of my life
And my tomorrows, all of which are in Thy hands,
The dark uncertain and unbearable hard days;
All of these days, too, are in Thy hands, O Lord.
So, because I am beloved of Thee,
I am content.
I lie there sleepless,
Yet fretless--and without care,
Because I am Thy child.

Date unknown

I remember the days of old;
I meditate on all thy works;
I muse on the work of thy hands.
I stretch forth my hands unto thee:
my soul *thirsteth* after thee,
as a thirsty land. Selah.
Psalm 143:5-6

Folio XIV--Prayer

Thank You for Trials

Thank you, Lord,
For the trials of life:
For dark days and shadows--
Yes, even the strife.
Thank you, Lord,
For the lessons I've learned:
For the rod and the stripe
In rebellion I earned.

I thank you, dear Lord,
That you taught me to pray
And drew me to read
Thy blest Book every day.
The day that you saved me
And claimed me as Thine
Will always to me be
My thanksgiving time.

**But he knoweth the way that I take:
when he hath tried me,
I shall come forth as gold.**
Job 23:10

Folio XV

Nature

The heavens declare the glory of God; and the firmament sheweth his handywork. Day unto day uttereth speech, and night unto night sheweth knowledge. *There is* no speech nor language, *where* their voice is not heard.
Psalm 19:1-3

Evening Hues

More beautiful
Than a painting
Is the sky I see tonight.
More lovely is its color
Than other evenings' sight.
The splendor of its purple,
The pinks and tints of gray
Seem to bring God's heaven closer
At the even time of day.

1966

Folio XV--Nature

The Sky at Evening

I like to see the sky at night
When the sun is sinking low;
I like to see the picture there
In evening's lovely glow.

I see in clouds a likeness
Of the dashing white foamed sea;
And as I watch this pretty view,
It seems to roll toward me.

I like to see the colors there
Of yellow, blue, and red
And to think about it later
When I lie upon my bed.

October 1958
This was written to my three grandsons after a walk one evening in Coral Heights, Florida.

Summer Time Is Here Again

The magic of Summer is here again,
And its sweetness fills the air.
The golden, living sunshine
Penetrates everywhere.

The trees in their party dresses
Raise coiffured heads to the sky.
While the wind, in flirtatious manner,
Seducingly passes by.

The air is thick with the fullness
Of Summers' laziness;
The drowsy drone of voices
Breaks into the silentness:

The persistent call of the birdling
As it waits for its mother's care;
The distant bark of a dog
Re-echoing everywhere.

It seems to me that summer
Is like life, when it is complete--
When there are no worlds to conquer,
No problems to defeat.

Folio XV--Nature

It seems that Mother Nature,
When the vigor of spring is spent,
Leans back in the comfort of summer
To rest with pleasant content.

1936
Written when we lived on Wager Avenue in Lakewood, Ohio.

For, lo, the winter is past, the rain is over *and* gone;
The flowers appear on the earth; the time of the singing *of birds* is come,
and the voice of the turtle[dove] is heard in our land;
The fig tree putteth forth her green figs,
and the vines *with* the tender grape give a *good* smell.
Song of Solomon 2:11-13a

Spring Is the Children's Season

Spring is the children's season
With the thrill of the new and clean.
The little ones view with wonder
The beauties they have seen:

The lure of the small green leaf,
The joy at the robin's song,
The mystery of the earth worm
As it slowly crawls along.

Yes, Spring is the children's season;
Their voices blend so well
With the soft clear notes of the song birds
As their throats with music swell.

The sun in so kindly manner
Shines down with its healthful rays,
Makes wonderful the days of Springtime
When the children come out to play.

1935
This was written to our children.

Folio XV--Nature

The Saucy Little Leaves

The saucy little leaves
Turned their backs one day
On their old friend the Wind,
Who was blowing by that way.

They flirted and they danced
And they sang a sweet refrain
And held up slender arms
To embrace the naughty rain.

But the Wind just moaned and sobbed
As he tossed them left and right,
Crying loudly he was robbed
Of the sweetness of his day.

Avenged he fled away;
He just couldn't bear to stay
And see those bruised and broken
Leaves upon the ground.

September 1942
This poem was written to the children.

Sunrise at Dawn

I awoke at dawn.
Perhaps it was His hand that stirred me
And sat before the East with clear, uncluttered view.
I saw the morn as it was born
From sky of blue and white and crimson
And was in awe before its wondrous hue.

Then as I watched and felt me in God's presence,
The sky arranged itself and changed so as to be
The background for the day of splendor,
Of the grandeur I was yet to see.

For there before my reverent vision,
I watched the sun appear and take command;
Its regal glory turning dawn to morning,
Giving light and life to all the land.

Before me mirrored in the lake, I watched this:
Each beauty picture with soft shadows too,
The trees so tall with graceful green palms waving,
The sky above in soft fresh virgin blue.

And then the sun in stately brilliance
Displayed its radiance in the water's face;
And my soul fell low before this demonstration
That God gives daily to the human race.

Folio XV--Nature

I praised that I, too, am His creation--
Made by the same great hand that made the sun;
Redeemed by Christ at such an obligation,
And saw the day as it had just begun.

May 1959
In St. Petersburg, Florida

📖

Cause me to hear thy lovingkindness in the morning;
for in thee do I trust:
cause me to know the way wherein I should walk;
for I lift up my soul unto thee.
Psalm 143:8

The Sky at Night

I like to see the sky at night
When the sun is going low.
I like to see the picture there
In evening's lovely glow.

I see in clouds a likeness
Of the rolling white foamed sea;
And as I watch this pretty view,
It seems to roll toward me.

I like to see the colors there
Of yellow, blue, and red;
And to think about it later
When I lie upon my bed.

October 1958
*This was written in Montgomery, Alabama, while remembering an evening when
I took a walk in Florida with young grandsons Don, Dave, and Dick.*

Folio XV--Nature

Trees I Know

We live where there are many trees
Where squirrels play among the leaves,
And wind a rushing sound does make
Like foamy waves upon the lake.

The trees, their stately heads hold high;
They seem to point us to the sky;
But we who marvel at the tree,
We look to God who made it be.

Those tall and sturdy ancient oaks
Are typical of many folks
Who firmly hold their place in life;
And growing upward out of strife
Send out assurance everywhere
Like oaks their branches in the air.

1935
*This was written while living on Wager Avenue (Lakewood, Ohio)
when the children were very young.*

With Tears in My Heart—the Poems of Gertrude Grace Sanborn

The Fading Flower

Its fragrance was just for the moment;
It lived thru the night and then died.
Its beauty was transient and fading;
Its fashion, not meant to abide.

It came from a seed to the blossom;
From its stem it soon fell to the earth,
Leaving none of its promising beauty
That was seen at the moment of birth.

Lord, let me not be like this flower,
For I would live more than one day
To pass on the fragrance of Heaven
To everyone passing this way.

1965
I was thinking of the Hibiscus flower.

Chinese hibiscus

Folio XV--Nature

They Bloom for Me

The flowers in my garden plot
Do grow for all to see;
And yet their lovely blossoms
Seem just to bloom for me.

Thru sun and rain or storm or wind
Tho bent and bruised they be,
They raise again their faces
And live awhile for me.

The flowers in my garden plot
Seem growing there for me,
And every pretty bud and leaf
Is waiting patiently.

I walk along my garden's path
And touch each petal rare,
So thankful for this beauty
Which I find living there.

July 1965

God's Winter

I look out from my window;
And there before my eyes
Are lovely fields of winter
Where snow so softly lies.

The vastness of this beauty
Upon each plane and hill,
The outline of the trees,
So black and bare and still

Just thrill my heart to praises!
Tis God who made it so.
He sends the times and seasons
To creatures here below.

1943

Folio XV--Nature

Morning in Winter

The sky overhead
Is gray in the dawn;
And the cold earth
Is snowy and white.
The slow moving morning
Is about to unveil
Itself and replace
Winter's night.

The trees looking gaunt--
Their black against gray,
The smoke from the chimney
Of the house 'cross the way,
The long winding road,
The milk truck with its load
Say "Morning in Winter" to me.

1943

With Tears in My Heart—the Poems of Gertrude Grace Sanborn

I Picked a Rose Today

I picked a rose today,
And I beheld its perfect beauty
With reverent ecstasy.
For God who makes each lovely rose
Makes it just for you and me.

I thought how thankless are we all
To take these gifts of grace
That in our garden bloom,
And never turn our hearts to praise
Or give Him room.

January, 1959

Folio XV--Nature

This Earth

This Earth that He made
Is so lovely,
From blue skies above
To the sod.
And I marvel to view
All this beauty,
This gift to my eyes
From our God.

What color! what splendor!
What wonder!
I gaze and my soul
Sings in praise;
No words from my lips
Can express it;
How great are His works
And His ways!

*The author wrote this poem while she was with her husband
on business trips in Georgia and Florida.*

The Rain and the Leaves

It was fall, and the leaves on the trees
Turned their silvery backs to the breeze;
They knew that the wind was displeased,
    But they longed for the rain.

The leaves, as they danced in delight,
Saw the clouds hide the sun from their sight;
They nodded from left to the right,
    For they knew it would rain.

They opened their arms to embrace
The rain as it kisses their green face;
They willingly stayed in their place
    And yielded to rain.

1942
To the children

Folio XV--Nature

A Rose

I walked into my garden
And looked upon a rose.
Ah, that a bloom could be so rare
One scarcely could suppose.

I gazed into the lovely flower
And wondered at each part.
Ah, that a bloom could come to be
From but a seedling start.

I smelled the fragrance it gave forth
And marveled and enjoyed
The mystic sweet perfumery
Which nature had employed.

Thus while my heart was speaking
And to my mind did say:
'Tis God who made this lovely rose
To see and smell today.

November 1961

September

What is so rare as a day in September?
Try as I will, I cannot remember
A time when the breezes were
So balmy and soft;
A day when the sun shone as
Gently aloft;
When trees their bright tint
Speak Autumn and fare,
Move great arms to shelter
And cover us there;
Grass green soft beneath me,
Blue skies over head
Repeating the question
of which I first said:
"Oh what is so rare as a day in September?"
So rare and so pleasant, I cannot remember!

September 1973

Folio XV--Nature

I Like the Rain!

I like the rain!
I like the way it make one feel
When it patters on the roof.
I like the way the sky gets grey,
The cloak it throws around the day,
The smell that fills the air someway.
I like the rain!

I like the rain!
I like the coziness at home
When I sit and meditate
Or read a book or sew or dream.
I like the rain; it makes me seem
Possessed and calm, and young and clean.
I like the rain!

1935

With Tears in My Heart—the Poems of Gertrude Grace Sanborn

A Yellow Rose

A fragile yellow rose
Picked from my garden today
Put in a vase of water
Set in a place for display.

Each petal so fragrantly scented
With color amazingly new
Even a yellow blossom
Gives witness what God can do.

1959

**I *am* the rose of Sharon,
and the lily of the valleys.**
Song of Solomon 2:1

Folio XV--Nature

Winter

When the snow is lying softly
On the ground
And here and there it drifts
Into a mound,
When trees are still and dark
Against a sky of gray
I know it's winter.

When in the morning
The sun withholds its rays
And snowbird twitter all around
At break of days,
When firesides glow
And call me there to dream,
I know it's winter.

While the earth remaineth,
seedtime and harvest,
and cold and heat,
and summer and winter,
and day and night shall not cease.
Genesis 8:22

With Tears in My Heart—the Poems of Gertrude Grace Sanborn

A Smile Is Like a Fragrant Rose

A thorny path I walk today
And oft I'm hurt and torn,
But here and there I find a rose
Tucked in between the thorn.

And tho the prick is sharp and keen
And I cry aloud in grief,
The pain is gone when I can see
A rose in sweet relief.

A friend, a smile, a word of cheer
To help me some hard day
Is like a lovely fragrant rose
Which blooms along the way.

July 30, 1949 and August 1961 (last verse)

Folio XV--Nature

I Walked Thru My Garden

I walked thru my garden one morning;
The flowers were bright in array.
Each one in its beautiful glory
Surpassed as I walked on my way.

I walked thru my garden at evening;
The flowers were wilted and dead.
And the beauty I saw in the morning
Had faded and vanished instead.

I wept as I walked thru my garden,
And I thought of my life now far spent;
And I wondered if it on the morrow
Would leave any beauty or scent.

I prayed as I went from my garden;
And cried unto God in the sky,
"Lord, let me not be like the flowers
To live for one day and then die."

June, 1965

With Tears in My Heart—the Poems of Gertrude Grace Sanborn

My Life Is Like a Garden Small

My life is like a garden small;
And flowers grow upon its wall,
Where lattice hold up bloom and vine
And leaves within their cause incline.

The workings of God's purpose great
Criss-crossed into my life
Are like the garden's lattice there
On which twine joy and strife.

A wall of circumstance and plan
Enclose my walk and way,
And I'm shut in to bring forth praise
To all who pass my way.

April 1958 and June 1962

And we know that
all things work together for good
to them that love God,
to them who are the called
according to his purpose.
Romans 8:28

Folio XV--Nature

I Am His Garden

I am His garden,
And He helps me to grow
That the fragrance of spices
Some others may know.

He calls for His winds
And on my garden doth blow
That the witness of Jesus
The lost world may know.

I am His garden
Where the sweet spices flow.
I am His planting;
He maketh me grow

In seasons of testing,
His North Wind doth flow
So that into this world
His witness must go.

March, 1984

Awake, O north wind; and come, thou south;
blow upon my garden, that the spices thereof may flow out.
Let my beloved come into his garden, and eat his pleasant fruits.
Song of Solomon 4:16

Folio
XVI

Audrey
June

I sought the LORD,
and he heard me,
and delivered me
from all my fears.
Psalm 34:4

My Little Mystery

She's a little bit big
And a little bit small,
A little bit short
And a little bit tall,
A little bit young
And a little bit old,
A little bit shy
And a little bit bold.

She's a little bit lady
And a little bit child,
A little bit calm
And a little bit wild,
A little bit naughty
And a little bit nice,
A little bit sugar
And a little bit spice.

She's a little bit dumb
And a little bit smart,
A little bit gracious
And a little bit tart,
A little bit sloppy
And a little bit neat,
A little bit sour
And a little bit sweet.

Folio XVI—Audrey June

She's a little bit prompt
And a little bit late,
Hair a little bit curly
And a little bit straight,
A little bit order
And a little bit muss,
A little bit patience
And a little bit fuss.

Just eleven years old and
And as precious as can be,
A little like her daddy
And a little like me!

1944 To Little Audrey June, age eleven

And the Syrians had gone out by companies, and had brought away captive out of the land of Israel a little maid; and she waited on Naaman's wife. And she said unto her mistress, Would God my lord *were* with the prophet that *is* in Samaria! for he would recover him of his leprosy.

2 Kings 5:2-3

Once I Had a Baby

I once had a dear little baby
Who was chubby and roguish and fair;
She sat on my lap, and I loved her
And sang as she cuddled there.

I sang of the moon and of Briar Fox;
I sang of our Father on high.
I sang to her songs about fairies,
And baby and "rock, rock a bye."

I think o'er the years, and I treasure
Each day and each year that I see;
For my wee little baby has grown up,
Too big now to sit on my knee.

I know it must be, and it's proper
For children to grow up to be
Too big to be sung to and cuddled,
And now she is singing to me.

You were my dear little baby.
You are still roguish and fair;
But O in my heart there's a longing
To still have you cuddle there.

1944
This was written to "June Bug," age twelve.
("June Bug" was a pet name for Audrey June who died in November of 1952.)

Folio XVI—Audrey June

To Audrey

God gave to my arms a girl baby
So perfect and healthy and dear;
We nourished and cherished her daily
And were always protectingly near.

She grew to a beautiful maiden
Quite lovely of face and form;
She charmed all who saw with her manner
So honest, so friendly, and warm.

Then our Father from Mansions of Glory
In wisdom that none can gainsay
Took from my arms this dear treasure
And enclosed her in His, one sad day.

November 1942
Audrey died at age twenty.

Naked came I out of my mother's womb, and naked shall I return thither:
the LORD gave, and the LORD hath taken away;
blessed be the name of the LORD.
Job 1:21

The Little Things

A flower she loved so well,
A dress in a window display,
A melody over the air,
A word that she used to say;

A night when the stars are bright,
One day when her friend passed by,
The chair on the lawn in the evening--
All bring a tear to my eye.

In church when I hear the organ,
A solo that she used to sing,
The place where she sat on Sunday,
A child like I used to bring;

Her favorite Scripture passage,
The ball game on that day,
Her raincoat hung in the closet,
A witty thing that she'd say;

Some beautiful antique china,
The first new robin of spring,
The smell of the grass in the mowing--
Such a longing do these things bring.

Folio XVI—Audrey June

A girl with golden tresses
In a roadster painted red,
The news in the local paper
That a friend of hers just wed--

It's the little things that bind me
To the years and days gone by.
It's the little things that hurt me so
And cause my heart to sigh.

May 1953
The author wrote this poem just before her daughter Audrey's birthday.
(Audrey June Sanborn had died about six months earlier.)

Jesus said unto her,
I am the resurrection, and the life:
he that believeth in me,
though he were dead,
yet shall he live:
And whosoever liveth and believeth in me
shall never die.
Believest thou this?
John 11:25-26

Her Room

I went up to her room one day
And looked into her drawers;
I opened up her cupboard
And peered into her stores.
I was so calm when I began
To sort and rearrange;
But as I touched her treasures,
My thoughts began to change.
The days gone by swept o'er me
Before she went away;
I had to stop and leave that room
Until another day.

Her hopes and dreams and treasures
There boxed in neat array
Bespoke her very presence
As I read what they did say.
The flowers for her lovely hair
And wisps of lacery
All made the room so vibrant
With her personality.

Folio XVI—Audrey June

In dresses hung so neatly,
Each in proper place--
I saw again her dear form
In all its girlish grace.
It broke my heart afresh,
And I took my eyes away;
I had to leave that empty room
And come another day.

I went up to His house that day
By means of fervent prayer;
I saw her all so lovely
Beside the golden stair.
Far better was the robe she wore
Than any cloth made here;
More lovely was reality
Than any dream held dear.
O Lord, just keep me looking
Up to that wondrous place;
And when my heart grows lonely here,
Turn there my eyes in Grace.

1953
This was written after Audrey's death at age twenty.

With Tears in My Heart—the Poems of Gertrude Grace Sanborn

Silly Little Shoes

Dear little silly shoes
That her graceful feet did wear--
She left them behind in the cupboard
In her room at the top of the stair.

Dear little "straps and heels"
Of black and blue and red--
She stepped from them into Heaven
And they mutely say,
"She is dead."

May 1953

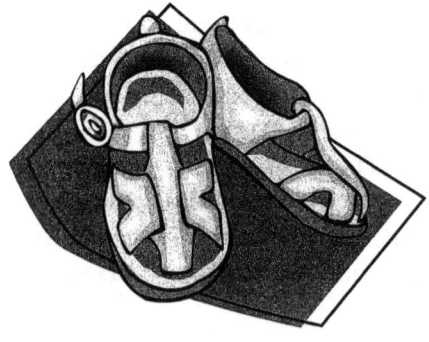

Folio XVI—Audrey June

I Never Thought That She Might Die

I never thought that she might die
So full of life was she;
So vibrant was the youth of her
With personality.

I never thought she'd waste away
Laid low by awful pain;
I never thought this child of mine
Would be so cruelly slain.

I never thought I'd helpless be
To do one thing that day,
To keep death's hands from reaching out
And taking her away.

March 1955
To Audrey who died at age twenty

**For this God *is* our God for ever and ever:
he will be our guide *even* unto death.**
Psalm 48:14

I Can Be Glad That She Has Gone

She has gone
And I did not want to lose her;
I would indeed have held her by the bands of love.
Torn from my side,
This little one I mothered,
Transported from our world to realms above.

I look around
And see the things that happen
To those who plan to live a full and happy life.
It grieves my heart to watch them disappointed.
I can be glad she's missed so much of strife.

She has gone
And I would not ask to have her
Come back again into this place of sin and care;
For safe is she from tempting tricks of Satan.
Though she's away, I'm glad God has her there.

April, 1955
written in Montreal

Folio XVI—Audrey June

To June

May was just becoming June
When she came to us,
Our lovely little flower.
We named her June,
With Hair of sunshine light
And eyes of springtime skies
And voice attune.

She stayed with us for twenty years
And brightened her own place
In our garden site;
Until one fall day,
A chilling blast
Closed her pretty petals fast.

May still slips into June each year,
And winter's winds the flowers kill.
Our lovely flower has gone,
But her fragrance still is here.
It is June all year.

June 1958

To My Little Girl

The lilac bush and the snowball tree
Are just as polite as bushes can be.
They bow low to the pine;
And they seem to agree,
By their nodding assent
That he is SOME tree.

The tall, stately pine
Just stands there--'tis true.
But he sways just a little
Toward the lilac of blue.
'Tis plain to be seen
She's really the queen
Of his heart.

To Mel

There on the altar of love, he bestowed
An offering so precious and fair--
A love quite untarnished with self or of gain,
So warm and unspotted and rare.

And Audrey, to whom it was offered
From its depths and its warmth and its length,
Was enabled to carry her burden
As she drew to herself of its strength.

This was written to Mel, the dear self-sacrificing young man whom Audrey loved--a man who stayed true to her to the end. (EDITOR: Though not dated, this poem must have been written in 1953 soon after the early death of the author's second-born daughter.)

Folio XVII

Beverly Grace

And the LORD said unto him,
Who hath made man's mouth?
or who maketh the dumb, or deaf,
or the seeing, or the blind?
have not I the LORD?
Exodus 4:11

When Baby's Sick

When baby's sick,
The clouds hang low;
And worries dark
Like shadows grow.
Black fears and dreads
Just come and go
When baby's sick.

When baby's sick,
The world's all wrong.
For me the bird
Has lost his song;
And those who laugh
Do not laugh long
When baby's sick.

The precious eyes
Which long for sleep
Are emphasized
With circles deep.
Her voice so weak
Just makes me weep
When baby's sick.

Folio XVII—Beverly Grace

Will joy again
Possess my heart?
Will I in life
Take up my part?
No use for me
A task to start
When baby's sick.

1937
The author wrote this poem when Beverly had pneumonia.
Beverly Grace was the third-born daughter of Ren and Gertrude Sanborn.
She was born with severe brain damage. This fact was unknown
to the author and her husband for several years.
Later in life, Beverly would suffer many bouts with adult pneumonia.

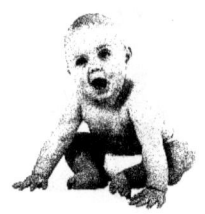

Baby Dear

Baby Dear, I love you so;
I could not love you more I know.
I love your eyes, so wide and wise
Deep blue reflections of the skies.

I love your mouth, so rosy sweet;
I love your little pink fat feet.
I love the work you cause for me;
For, Baby Dear, you're mine you see.

1935
This is the author's first poetic effort. It was written to daughter Beverly before Gertrude learned that her child was brain injured at birth.

Folio XVII—Beverly Grace

The Lightning Bug

When the time comes 'round at the end of day,
The lightning bugs come out to play;
And a sweet little girl, whose name I know,
Just loves to watch them gleam and glow.

The lightning bug has a very fine light,
And he flies around 'most all of the night.
He goes so high to the tree tops round,
And then swoops down to the dew wet ground.

His lights glows brightly, and his light glows dim
While the sweet little girl runs after him.
He's a very funny fellow; and I don't know where he lives,
Or how he goes about to make the light he gives.

1940
To Beverly Grace

With Tears in My Heart—the Poems of Gertrude Grace Sanborn

My Precious Little Half Chick

I have a little treasure
Most too rare to tell by pen;
She's my precious little "Half Chick"
And her years are nearly ten.

She cannot talk, nor understand;
She was born that way, you see.
And she's twined around this heart of mine
Her dear infirmity:

The tears I've shed, the black long nights,
The hopeless endless fears,
The anguish of a mother's heart,
The fruitless empty years.

I turned one day to His dear face;
I placed her in His care.
I do not dread the coming years
Nor find the load still there.

For He sent this little treasure--
Too dear for line or pen,
This precious little "Half Chick"
Whose years are nearly ten.

1944
This poem was used in the booklet <u>Able to Bear It</u>.

Folio XVII—Beverly Grace

My Precious Problem

Grace that He lets me have it;
Marvel He trusts me so;
Always He helps me bear it
Because He loves me so.

Strange are His ways to show me;
His way and His power and peace;
But perfect His manner and method
To bring for a sure increase.

Light are the daily duties
And tender my work of love
While I care for my precious problem
Because it is one I love.

Dear little precious problem
That God has given to me;
Twined round my very being
Her poor infirmity.

Gladly in love I serve her
And all of her weakness bear;
My dear little precious burden
Whom God has put in my care.

1952
"My heart and my strength for both of my precious weak ones."

Helpless

Sickness has touched my dear one;
Disease has taken control.
Pain has encompassed her body;
Weakness in great surges rolls.

Helpless I am as I sit here
Holding her hot hand in mine
Praying "My Father, please heal her!"
Wanting not His will but mine.

Yearning to help, yet so helpless;
Unable to do aught but wait;
Wondering how I have failed her;
Allowing her health to abate.

Hours I sit here just watching.
The Lord has been speaking to me
And turning my doubts into trusting
No matter what His will may be.

May 1956
This was written when Beverly was ill in Albany, Georgia.

Folio XVII—Beverly Grace

I Wonder Why?

Torn is my heart still
As I gaze in the face
Of my poor little child
Named Beverly Grace.

So void of maturity
Wisdom or thought,
Never to learn
And never be taught.

Years now are added
And days have fled by
And--tho not in rebellion--
I still wonder, "Why?"

February 19, 1959
The author wrote this poem on the twenty-fourth birthday
of her retarded daughter Beverly.

Dear Little Strange One

How I love thee, dear little strange one--
Heart of my very heart,
Drawing from me
The strength for your life,
Clinging to every part.

How I love thee, dear little strange one--
Born thru my hours of pain,
Child with such loss
Becoming my cross,
My grief and my tears,
Yet my gain.

How I love thee, dear little strange one--
Burns in my soul such a fire,
Devotion intense,
A mother's incense,
Compelling and yearning desire.

1973
This was written to daughter Beverly Grace.

Folio XVII—Beverly Grace

Lost and Strayed Away

Stark fear and terrible terror
Hold both my heart and mind.
I wept with deepest pleading;
Pray God would quickly find
My helpless, hopeless frail one
Who is lost and strayed away;
She's deaf and mute and helpless
And cannot find her way.

Oh Lord, dear Lord, please bring her
Once more unto my arms;
The care of her seems nothing
So great are my alarms.
Dear Father, find my weak one;
I am so crushed with pain;
And when I hold my darling,
I'll not complain again.

August 18, 1973
Daughter Beverly, who was severely retarded,
wandered away and was gone for about one hour.
The Collingwood, New Jersey police found her.

With Tears in My Heart—the Poems of Gertrude Grace Sanborn

Bless the Day

Bless the day
When she came to me,
The dear little broken thing,
Needing my strength,
My heart, my life--
Dependent for everything.

Bless the day
When she broke my heart,
And I knew she would
Never be normal;
And the tears did flow
Until I came to know
That God permitted this sorrow.

June 1986

Creep Mouse and Pinch Bug

The creep mouse and the pinch, pinch bug
Scheme and try for a big, big hug.
They creep and creep toward the baby's face
To find a soft, soft pinching place.

They walk so slowly with steps so high
On soft fat legs as they go by.
And about this time, in the creep mouse race,
They come upon the cuddling place.

They creep up close to the laughing face
And put a pinch on the pinching place.
They walk so quick up the round pink cheeks
And give the baby's ear a tweak.

They dance upon the baby's nose,
A tiny thing that breathes and blows.
And then they jump with all their might
And hug the laughing baby tight.

*This was a game the author
played with her daughters
when they were little babies.*

Folio XVIII

Children

Lo, children *are* an heritage of the LORD:
and the fruit of the womb *is his* reward.
As arrows *are* in the hand of a mighty man;
so *are* children of the youth.
Happy *is* the man that hath his quiver full of them:
they shall not be ashamed,
but they shall speak with the enemies in the gate.
Psalm 127:3-5

With Tears in My Heart—the Poems of Gertrude Grace Sanborn

A Lonely Journey

I took a lonely journey
Into the Valley of Pain;
And each time from this place of anguish,
As I came forth again and again,
I held in my hand a child's hand
And started a small new life
Out on the Roadway of Living
And into the Highway of Strife.

The date is unknown.
The author gave birth to three daughters.
Beverly's birth was extremely difficult.
It was during the birthing process that Beverly's brain was damaged causing
her to be retarded--not able to talk, etc. all of her life.

Lo, children *are* an heritage of the LORD:
***and* the fruit of the womb *is his* reward.**
Psalm 127:3

Folio XVIII--Children

My Garden

In songs, they sing of gardens of the heart.
There are stories long of other gardens too.
But I've a lovely garden
Where children live and grow
And blossom into flowers
With brilliant colors glow.
They've been watered with affection;
In tenderness they grew.
As their little personalities
Came shyly peeping through,
We breathe their fragrance--
Sweet with childish joy.
We hold their beauty closely to our hearts;
Their years mature before our view.
The winds of season bring us
Their joys and sorrows--hues
Of these precious flowers
That we are tending to.
Now some folks dream of painting lovely views
While others long for gold or worldly fame;
But I dream of my garden
Where children live and grow,
And thank God for the blessings
That only Gardeners know.

February 1935
This was written after Beverly was born and before we knew she was retarded.

Crying Babies Ringing Phones

Crying babies
Ringing phones
Buzzing door bells
Washer's drone.

Baker's whistle
Ash man's call
Frantic mother
Hears them all.

Chatter, clatter
Pitter pat
Children pushing
This and that.

Pounding blocks
And window knocks
Paper tearing
Jumpers daring.

Banging bottles
Babies fall
Running feet
Bumps on wall.

Folio XVIII--Children

Hurry, hurry
On the run
Dashing, darting
Get things done.

Noises, noises
Everywhere
In the head
And in the air.

Smacking lips
Rumbling tummies
Children's voices
"Mummy, Mummy."

Little voices
Are so dear
As they fall
Upon my ear.

Mother giving
Getting too
Love and loving
Things to do.

Planning, thinking
As they grow
Dreams for each
I love them so.

1935
This was written around 1935 on Wager Avenue
in Lakewood, Ohio when Beverly was a small baby.

I Wonder

I wonder when we're old and gray
How thing will be with us,
And if we'll cause our children
Perplexities and fuss.

I wonder if we'll relive,
As old folks often do,
And talk of all the days before
And trials we've been thru.

Do you suppose my hair will be
A lovely silver gray?
Or will it fade and streaked be
In an ugly sort of way?

Will husband's step be firm in stride,
Or will he have become
A worn and weary stooping man
Who leans on everyone?

Will I be kind and friendly
And think with open mind?
Or will I grow cross and narrow,
And to youth and life be blind?

Will our children's children
Bring happiness complete?
Or will their cool indifference
Bring sadness and defeat?

1936
The author wrote this poem when she was thirty-two.

Folio XVIII--Children

A Threefold Blessing

Now I am a mother, a daughter, and wife;
And I live a most varied and intricate life.
I must not love Mother with all of my heart,
Or Hubby'd get mad and a quarrel would start.

And if I show children devotion intense,
My mother might say it was silly nonsense.
And if to my hubby I'm sweet as can be,
The children all cry, "Why don't you love me?"

But since I'm a mother, a daughter, and wife
And must live this varied and intricate life,
I'll write oft to Mother and tell how I care;
I'll keep house for Hubby and wait for him there;
I'll cuddle the children and teach them to know
The things they should learn to develop and grow.

I'll be to Mother as sweet as can be;
I'll be to hubby what he is to me.
Three precious pathways all laid out to be;
Three avenues of blessing intended for me.

1939

They've Gone

They've gone--
The children and their dad.
The house is very quiet and just a little sad.
The rush, rush, rush, is over;
And they've gone to work and school
To earn the daily money
And to learn of book and rule

They've gone--
The children and their dad.
I know it by the things that lie around:
The puzzle on the table
To be worked again tonight,
A magazine with pages rolled,
Newspapers left and right,
Pajamas in the bedroom, and
Slippers in the hall,
One bed neat and tidy,
And one not made at all.
Empty cups and sticky spoons
And crusts of toast I see
Still upon the table
Which they left so hurriedly.

Folio XVIII--Children

Yes, they've gone--
The children and their dad.
How precious tho to serve them and
To try to make them glad;
So I will clean up all the dishes,
And I'll set the house to right;
And leave the puzzle on the table
To be worked again tonight.

1943

Bright Gems

Bright gems
In a golden setting--
Our children
Set in Thy love,
The finest gift
I can offer
To Thee,
My Father above.

1944

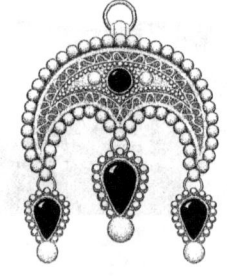

Folio XVIII--Children

Our Gems

Spirit of God, I give to Thee
These Jewels in my arms.
I know that Thou wilt guard them
And keep them from all harms.

Spirit of God, I give to Thee
The care of treasures rare.
Just set them for Thy glory
And radiance anywhere.

1944

📖

And they shall be mine,
saith the LORD of hosts,
in that day when I make up my jewels;
and I will spare them,
as a man spareth his own son that serveth him.
Malachi 3:17

Memories

Many days with gladness
Many nights with song;
Many hours of joyfulness
Glad the whole day long.

Times of carefree laughter
Time of youth and life;
All the world seemed mine,
And there was no strife.

Times with children's voices
Filled the home with glee;
All the happy hours
Come rushing back to me.

Days of great revival
In my heart to God;
When I gave Him all
Whom to Calvary trod.

Seasons of abundance
Times of want and lack;
All this comes before me now
As now my thoughts turn back.

Folio XVIII--Children

Now the days are harder,
And the nights are long.
Now the road is rougher,
And I'm not as strong.

All the care of living
Try to cloud my mind.
And the joys of yesteryear
Seem so far behind.

But I praise the Father
For everyday now past;
Since it helps me live for him
While the living lasts.

November 1951

I count all things *but* loss
for the excellency of the knowledge
of Christ Jesus my Lord:
for whom I have suffered the loss of all things,
and do count them *but* dung, that I may win Christ,
Philippians 3:8

Folio XIX

My Husband

But be ye doers of the word,
and not hearers only,
deceiving your own selves.
For if any be a hearer of the word, and not a doer,
he is like unto a man beholding his natural face in a glass:
For he beholdeth himself, and goeth his way,
and straightway forgetteth what manner of man he was.
But whoso looketh into the perfect law of liberty, and continueth *therein*,
he being not a forgetful hearer, but a doer of the work,
this man shall be blessed in his deed.
James 1:22-25

With Tears in My Heart—the Poems of Gertrude Grace Sanborn

To Daddy

Here's to the children's Daddy--
A kiss for his dear, kind face.
A loud hurrah for the manner
He fills the father's place.

A cheer for the way he shoulders
The burdens we impose;
And great respect to Daddy
For the business things he knows.

A "thank you dear" from Mother
For the way he helps to share
The work of home and children
The perplexities and care.

Here's to the children's Daddy
A kiss for his dear, kind face.
We send a prayer of blessing
Straight up to the Throne of Grace.

Father's Day, 1935
This was the year that Beverly, the third-born daughter, was born.

Folio XIX—My Husband

To My Dear One

I'm glad, my love,
That we can be together.
I pray, my dear,
That you will always care.
I'm thankful, too,
For happiness you've brought me--
For joy and sorrow that we
Both can share.

I do not long
For costly homes or servants
Or plans where riches have a part.
I long to be
Your loving life companion;
For I love you, dear,
With all my heart.

1936
To "Buddy" (the author's husband)

**Likewise, ye husbands,
dwell with *them* according to knowledge,
giving honour unto the wife, as unto the weaker vessel,
and as being heirs together of the grace of life;
that your prayers be not hindered.**
1 Peter 3:7

Think of Me

Think of me when the sun shines
As if it were my smile.
Think of me when the rain falls
As I wept once a while.

Think of me when it's morning
When I was gay and young and free.
Think of me in the twilight;
But, Dearest, think of me.

1940
The author wrote this to her husband whom she affectionately called "Buddy."

**Think upon me, my God, for good,
according to all that I have done for this people.**
Nehemiah 5:19

Folio XIX—My Husband

Missed

He had hardly gone
When I began to miss him--
Just closed the door
And said goodbye to me.
I scarce had heard the words,
When I began to wish him
Just starting Home
And coming back to me.

1955
This was written to "R. O.," her husband.

📖

Thou shalt be missed,
because thy seat will be empty.
1 Samuel 20:18b

With Tears in My Heart—the Poems of Gertrude Grace Sanborn

Steadfast and Unmoveable

My husband has a favorite verse,
And you can plainly tell
Which part of it he likes the best
And keeps so very well.
He is steadfast and unmoveable!

No matter how you plead the case
No wavering you'll find.
Now Webster calls it firmness--
And this I really like--
But the term I use to call it
He surely doesn't like!

In Christian circles, we do say
Be steadfast and abounding;
But husband is so stubborn
I can't help this resounding!

That he is quite unmoveable
Is also plain to see,
For I can not deter his plan
By any tear or plea!

He's abounding here,
And abounding there,
And labors to distraction--
Until he's tired and weary
And has a bad reaction!

Folio XIX—My Husband

He overdoes in everything--
Excess is what he aims for--
Be steadfast and unmoveable
Is just the state he strains for!

For one to be industrious
Is worthy of much praise;
But he is so abounding
He's shortening his days!

Now in this favorite verse of his,
It plain and clear does state
The 15th of Corinthians
And last verse, fifty-eight!

That steadfastness in service
And standing in the fight,
Together with abounding,
Is always good and right!
(I must say verse fifty-eight
Is good for one to emulate.)

July 1, 1961

**Therefore, my beloved brethren, be ye stedfast, unmoveable,
always abounding in the work of the Lord,
forasmuch as ye know that your labour is not in vain in the Lord.**
1 Corinthians 15:58

Folio XX

Yvonne

Humble yourselves therefore
under the mighty hand of God,
that he may exalt you in due time:
Casting all your care upon him;
for he careth for you.
Be sober, be vigilant; because your adversary the devil,
as a roaring lion, walketh about, seeking whom he may devour:
Whom resist stedfast in the faith,
knowing that the same afflictions are accomplished
in your brethren that are in the world.
But the God of all grace, who hath called us
unto his eternal glory by Christ Jesus,
after that ye have suffered a while,
make you perfect, stablish, strengthen, settle *you*.
To him *be* glory and dominion for ever and ever. Amen.

1 Peter 5:6-11

The King's Daughter

The King--immortal, eternal,
The ruler of Heaven and earth--
Has left me the care of His daughter
Since the day of her spiritual birth.

She was born one day thru believing
In Jesus, the Son of His love;
She now is one of His family;
Her citizenship is above.

She lives here a pilgrim, a stranger,
A princess, joint heir, with His Son,
To grow up in wisdom and knowledge
Until her short stay here is done.

The King gave a Book of Instructions
For type, admonition, and thought;
He expects me to see that she learns them
And to see that she's carefully taught.

A wonderful, wonderful privilege
The King has given to me
To teach her the language of Heaven
And to walk and behave mannerly.

Folio XX--Yvonne

You are this princess, my daughter;
You're fair as the morning to me.
You're sweet as the fragrance of flowers;
"All glorious within" you must be.

October 1942
This was written to the author's first-born child Yvonne, age fifteen.

The king's daughter *is* all glorious within:
her clothing *is* of wrought gold.
She shall be brought unto the king in raiment of needlework:
the virgins her companions that follow her shall be brought unto thee.
With gladness and rejoicing shall they be brought:
they shall enter into the king's palace.
Instead of thy fathers shall be thy children,
whom thou mayest make princes in all the earth.
I will make thy name to be remembered in all generations:
therefore shall the people praise thee for ever and ever.
Psalm 45:13-17

A Little Talk

I'd like to talk a little while
To you, my daughter dear,
About the way to look at life;
So listen close and hear.

I walked along these very roads;
I hear you say, "That's odd
That Mom should know a road
That I have never trod!"

But life is much the same for all,
And folks no different act;
So let me pass along some helps
And believe that they are fact!

I'd like to have you take each day
As a clean and brand new page;
You'll find this thought a blessing
No matter what your age.

That you may see in each day's store
Things interesting and gay,
That you can find enjoyment
Along a common way.

Folio XX--Yvonne

Make conversation with a child
As he walks the path with you;
Enjoy his childish prattle--
It will thrill and startle you.

If you will kind to old folks be,
You'll be repaid in treasure;
For I have found in older ones
The choicest kind of pleasure.

A little nod, a word of cheer
To someone gray and tired
Will brighten up their eyes,
And leave you most inspired.

Do learn to laugh at many things
And let folks laugh with you;
You'll find so little that's unkind
And meant for hurting you.

Lift your eyes to view God's work
And in each season change;
See lovely fields of winter
Or summer's green arranged.

(continued on next page)

(continued from previous pages)

Enjoy the trees so cold and bare
Against the icy sky,
All crystal clear with shininess
Presented for your eye.

Or thrill to Autumn's colors
Or Spring's new green and rain.
And revel in the summer;
A poet's soul you'll gain.

You will find, my daughter dear,
That God will walk with you.
He's been on all my journeys,
And I know He'll take you thru.

There'll be no day that's dark or dull,
Or time that seems in vain
If you make each day adventure,
And from it lessons gain.

To Daughter Vonnie (Yvonne), age seventeen

Folio XX--Yvonne

I Wish That I Could Weep for You

I wish that I could weep for you
The tears that you will shed.
I wish that I could take myself
The sorrows on ahead.

I wish there were a way
To go before you, dear--
Solve your every problem
And put away each fear.

I wish that simply loving
Could lighten every load--
Make your life a pleasant one
As you travel on its road.

1945
To Vonnie

At Night When You Were Little

At night when you were little
And were fast asleep in bed,
I'd step into your quiet room
And pat your golden head.
I'd look upon your little face,
And kiss your sweet soft cheek,
And tuck the covers round you there
And take a good night peek.

I'd love to do the same thing now,
But it seems I do intrude;
So I do not op' the door at night
Because you'd think it rude.
I'd love to tuck the covers in
The same old loving way,
And kiss your cheek a few more times
Before you go away.

1945
To the author's oldest daughter Yvonne before she left for Bible school.

Gone Away

She went away and left us;
She's off with Book and rule
To learn to live and labor
In a distant Bible school.

She's packed up her belongings
And put them in a case.
And now her cupboard's empty,
And she's left a lot of space.

She took her hats and stockings
And her skirts and blouses too.
She took her shoes and dresses
And, of course, her curlers too.

She made it quite a problem
When she packed her clothes and sox.
She filled up all the luggage
And then she filled a box.

She's gone and home is different;
But I'm glad that she could go
To learn and live the Scripture
And to work and pray and grow.

I'm praying God will use her
In this world so dark with sin.
It's a precious gift I've given
When I gave this child to Him.

January 1946
To Yvonne, when she left for Moody Bible Institute in Chicago

God's College

I'm going to school in God's college
To train 'til eternity's day;
To get my degree in life's service,
The Lord Jesus is paying my way.

So I study and work in my classes
And advance from the low to the high
While my school term is nearing completion
And my vacation is due in the sky.

One day I will be at commencement,
And nail pierced hands will take mine
When I rise and receive my diploma
And enter Eternity's climb.

1946
The author's oldest daughter was away at Bible school in 1946.

Folio XX--Yvonne

First Born

Longed for and loved
Before she was formed
Yearned for, desired
Before she was born;
None other quite like her
So close to my heart
Is my love for the first born.
So precious thou art.

March 1960
to "Vonnie," my first-born

But he shall acknowledge . . . the firstborn,
by giving him a double portion
of all that he hath:
for he *is* the beginning of his strength;
the right of the firstborn *is* his.
Deuteronomy 21:17

Strange That I, Your Mother

Strange that I, your mother,
Should in my sorrow be
So blind that I have not seen
Your tears of memory.

Strange that I should overlook,
Have thought I wept apart
Or missed our precious Dear One
Alone within my heart.

I should have known, dear daughter,
How deeply you are grieved
To have lost your sister
And been so much bereaved.

So then, shall we together
With reverence wonder "why?"
While in our hearts deep recess,
We both for her do cry.

Until that day He calls us
And we see her by His side,
We must leave the "why?" with Jesus
And trustingly abide.

June 1961
written to Yvonne

Folio XX--Yvonne

His Cup in the Sack

Innocent and precious,
Yet having a lack,
God's silver cup
Was put into her sack.

Though hard to accept,
God knoweth what's best
When He uses our DEAR ONE
With His cup for a test.

Lord, how I marvel
At Thy purpose and plan
To use Thine own cup
To touch hearts of man.

One day He will tell us
His reasons and why
He touches our children
And makes our hearts cry.

There is a "cup in the sack" in every family--a silver cup, sometimes put there by the Lord.
(Genesis 44:2, 12)

Folio XXI

My Mother

The hoary head
is a crown of glory,
if it be found
in the way
of righteousness.
Proverbs 16:31

My Mother

She goes by the name of mother
And of "mumsy" now and then.
Brother calls her "Mom"
And sister calls her "Jen."

She is neat and soft and "iggy."*
Her eyes are nice warm brown;
She looks so smart and classy
When she's fixed to go down town.

I'm proud to have this mother,
And gladness fills my heart.
But when I take my pen in hand,
I don't know where to start.

Into the deep dark valley
Where all the mothers go,
Tarried there my mother
So four of us could grow.

She smiles when we have happiness
And cries when we have tears.
She always says we're wonderful
No matter what her fears.

This is a thought for "Mother"
On this day that's set apart.
There's no one else like you, Dear,
And I love you with all my heart.

a "family word" meaning "loveable"
This was written about 1937 – "To Mom on Mother's Day."

My Mother's Kitchen

Row upon row on shelves so neat
Were deftly arranged such things to eat
As sugar and spice and coffee and tea;
Fresh paper scallops peep over each row
While the door of each cupboard
Have windows that glow;
Floors slick and shining and curtains so neat,
A table well set with good things to eat;
A sink white with scrubbing, a place for the broom--
I love to remember each thing in that room.
A tall kitchen cabinet with place wide and clean
To put fresh baked pies of choc'late and cream,
Warm bread on racks and coffee cake too,
Hot biscuits in rings and poppy seed things
In my Mother's kitchen.

1940

A Household Engineer

In this scientific era
Of specialty and fame,
Only those who work and rate it
Are given great acclaim.

So I'll step up to the platform,
Tho there be no cry nor cheer,
And demand my hard earned letter
As a household engineer.

There's the project of the laundry,
With its soap and suds and foam,
And the project of the bucket
That makes a bight clean home.

There are formula and data
That go into pie and cake,
And delicious "science" secrets
That only Mom can make.

And don't forget the children
Those who are my task to rear
With love and care and labor
Of the household engineer.

1949

Folio XXI—My Mother

Understanding

I thought I understood
When your Dear One left that day.
I stood by you and grieved with you
And wiped your tears away.

Then came to me such sorrow
When my Dear One said "goodbye."
I understood your grief, dear heart,
Since such a loss have I.

May 1953
The author has inscribed this poem, "To My Mother."
Her mother was Jenny Barker whose oldest son died at the age of twenty-five.

O death, where *is* thy sting?
O grave, where *is* thy victory?
The sting of death *is* sin;
and the strength of sin *is* the law.
But thanks *be* to God,
which giveth us the victory
through our Lord Jesus Christ.
1 Corinthians 15:55-57

Folio XXII

Father

Let all things be done decently and in order.
1 Corinthians 14:40

To My Father

Father dear, I love you;
I love your furrowed brow.
I have a tender feeling
Coming o'er me even now.

All the good things I'll remember--
The very way you look.
Your heart desires to serve Him;
You love the precious Book.

I love to hear you singing
The songs too hard and high,
To watch each facial movement
The way you close your eye.

I cherish every manner--
All the songs you taught to me,
The way you played the keyboard;
Everything is dear to me.

You are very funny, Father,
And you show a ready wit.
You are clever with your pencil
And can draft a goodly skit.

Folio XXII--Father

You always work by blueprint;
You know your way is better--
A stickler for a theory,
An adherent to the letter.

These few thoughts I write to you,
Tho there are many more.
As years roll on and days go by,
I love you more and more!

1940

Children, obey your parents
in the Lord:
for this is right.
Honour thy father and mother;
(which is the first commandment with promise;)
That it may be well with thee,
and thou mayest live long on the earth.
And, ye fathers,
provoke not your children to wrath:
but bring them up in the nurture and admonition of the Lord.
Ephesians 6:1-4

Sickness

My days are made heavy;
My thoughts are made sad
When I think I shall soon
Say farewell to my Dad.

How can I e'er meet it
And say my goodbyes
And look for the last time
Into his dear eyes?

To see him so sickened
And wasted and old,
I ache with compassion
Too deep to be told.

To hear his voice weaken
Just breaks my sad heart.
How can I so spare him?
How can we thus part?

The years now seem priceless
That I took lightly and gay;
And I cling to each moment
And hour of today.

I look on his face,
And I hold close to me
His dear fading image
That's so precious to me.

1949
The author's father, Herbert Charles Barker, died January 1950.

Folio XXII--Father

Flag of Our Honor

My heart stirs within me.
The flag passes by
Or waves from a standard
And floats in the sky.

Its majestic colors
One thankfully sees.
With graceful unfurlings
It floats in the breeze.

I love this dear symbol
Of union and power.
I never so loved it
As I do this hour.

Though presidents falter
And leaders may fall,
Yet still this blest banner
Must fly over all.

I pray for our country,
Fair home of the free.
O grant us brave leaders
Who love liberty!

Dear flag of our honor
Brave emblem of fame,
God keep it free-flying
To ne'er dip in shame!

Folio XXIII

Other Family Members

God setteth the solitary in families.
Psalm 68:6a

Grandma's House

It was fun to go to Grandmas!
There was so much to eat.
She always gave us presents
And told us we were sweet.

Such fun to go to Grandmas!
It was the cleanest place,
With bright and shining windows
Hung with curtains trimmed in lace.

It was fun to go at Christmas
When everyone would come.
We'd have all kind of goodies
And have the best of fun.

Yes, 'twas fine to visit Grandma
When you were very small.
It still is nice at her house
But we never go at all.

I don't have a Grandma now;
They both have gone away.
But I'm glad that I remember
In this special sort of way.

1939
written to the author's two grandmothers, Maria Castle & Jane Kemp Barker

Folio XXIII—Other Family Members

I Had a Little Brother

I had a little brother once
With eyes so very blue
Whose hair was gold and silvery
And curled as hair should do.

I had a little brother once
Who grew to be a man
Whose hair was slick and masculine;
Imagine if you can.

A fine young man of twenty-five
So full of plans to live,
So clean and strong
But not for long.

God laid His hand upon this lad
And took him home one day,
And now his sister's very sad
Because he's gone away.

1937
To Richard Barker, the author's brother who died in 1931 at the age of 25

📖

**Therefore *we are* always confident, knowing that,
whilst we are at home in the body, we are absent from the Lord:**
2 Corinthians 5:6

With Tears in My Heart—the Poems of Gertrude Grace Sanborn

Thus Have I Loved Thee

All thru the years
Prayed for with tears
Watching with fears
I have loved thee.

On many days
Thru varied ways
In step or delays
I have loved thee.

In thought by thy side
Whatever betide
Yearning to guide
Have I loved thee.

Wanting God's best
Observing each test
In lag or in zest
I have loved thee.

In fellowship sweet
With thee at His feet
In worship so sweet
Thus have I loved thee.

September 1963
To my son-in-law Don for whom I pray

Folio XXIII—Other Family Members

A Wonderful Thing

A wonderful thing has happened to me
Banishing life's monotony,
Bringing me fresh and newest of joys--
This wonderful thing of three little boys.

Tho they belong to other arms,
Still I may revel in their charms.
Each day more dear they grow to be--
These three little boys so precious to me.

I was not asked, nor could I say
If they might come across my way;
But now they're here and have captured my heart.
They seem of myself a very large part.

Why do I think of them each day
While they are many miles away?
Why do I yearn to see each face,
Feeling their arms in childish embrace?

Now I am sure 'tis nothing new.
This has happened before to quite a few--
To become Grandma to three little boys
All full of vigor and vim and noise.

March 23, 1955
Written in Montreal, Canada

The Bride

So happy and glad
With no thought of sorrow
Thinking today will be
Just like tomorrow.

Eager and trusting
With great things to do
Submissive and yielding
Love's will to do.

Thrilled to be living
Glad she was born
Laughing at problems
Never forlorn.

Like a flower unfolding
In petals of lace
A sweet lovely virgin
With veil on her face.

With diamond and rings
Her hands held in his
Give vows for a lifetime
How solemn it is!

Folio XXIII—Other Family Members

By God unite
Who them did create
Made one by His edict
An Holy Estate.

June 1976
To Granddaughter Audrey Dianne on her wedding day, August 27, 1976.

📖

Can a maid forget her ornaments, *or* a bride her attire?
Jeremiah 2:32a

With Tears in My Heart—the Poems of Gertrude Grace Sanborn

A Little Child Can

A little child can love Him;
A little child can pray.
A little child can trust Him
And learn His Word each day.

A little child can praise Him
And show his friends the Way.
A little child can live for God
And serve Him every day.

1964
Written to that author's only granddaughter, Audrey Dianne, age seven.

**Even a child is known by his doings,
whether his work *be* pure, and whether *it be* right.**
Proverbs 20:11

Folio XXIII—Other Family Members

Kristen

Petal soft skin
Fair silken hair
Dark melting eyes
Turned everywhere.

Dear clinging arms
Hands, small, adept
Strong little legs
Feet firmly set.

Soft graceful body
In min'ature form
Grace in each movement
Small girl in the norm.

Oh, how we love her
This woman to be
This baby-sized person
Sweet Kristen Cosby.

By Great Grandma Sanborn
March, 1983

Folio XXIV

Christian Life

Thou therefore, my son,
be strong in the grace
that is in Christ Jesus.
And the things
that thou hast heard of me
among many witnesses,
the same commit thou to faithful men,
who shall be able to teach others also.
2 Timothy 2:1-2

Learning to Trust God

Learning to trust Him day by day
Learning to walk this pilgrim way
Learning to stay firm in the fray
Learning to stand true to Jesus.

Learning to tell the story sweet
Learning to sit before His feet
Learning to pose upon His breast
Learning to lean in wondrous rest.

Learning His precious Word each day
Learning to live as He doth say
Learning to pray in everything
Learning my cares and hopes to bring.

Learning to cry, yet not despair
Learning to love and how to share
Learning to lead, yet not to rule
Learning my lessons in His school.

Learning to wait with longing more
Learning this life may soon be o'er
Learning my times are in His hands
Learning this life my Lord commands.

Folio XXIV—Christian Life

El Shaddai

For years I have looked for a place I could rest
To pillow my head on a comforting breast,
And to lose all my cares, simply put them away,
And breathe in the air of a burdenless day.

I've longed so to hide from each problem I see,
From each tug at my heart that this life's brought to me.
How I've wanted to flee and to lie down to sleep
And forget that I e'er had a duty to keep.

But I've found not a place nor a refuge to hide
Where I could unload all the grief that's inside;
Till one day I read in the BOOK so divine,
And the Spirit put joy in this weak heart of mine.

For He showed me a place
Where it said I could rest
'Neath the Wings of EL SHADDAI
On the warmth of His breast.

Genesis 17:1; 1 Corinthians 6:18
1937

God Abideth Faithful

No friend can bring you constant friendship;
Nor son nor daughter
Can bring perfect love to thee.
No thing can bring thee satisfaction,
No place a haven really be.

Trust not in child nor friend or situation;
Trust not in human minds so frail.
Place neither love nor adoration
In things of earth and clay
To no avail.

When thru times of tears and disappointment,
Things we thought were good
Have turned to clay;
God the Father turns our eyes on Jesus
And He stands there waiting every day.

He alone is Altogether Lovely,
Never fails, betrays, nor turns aside,
Cannot change--not even just a shadow.
Tho we fail, He constant does abide.

Hard it is to feel alone, unwanted;
Hurt we are to see others take our place;
Helpless as we find no helper present;
Just now, dear soul, look up to Jesus' face.

2 Timothy 2:13
1944
Only Jesus is faithful forever!

Folio XXIV—Christian Life

Be Not Discouraged

Do not be discouraged
As along life's road you walk,
When things all point to failure
And it hurts your heart to talk.

When those you thought were loyal
Proved the same as all the rest;
And there seemed to be no person
Who would really stand the test.

It's hard to learn that people
Do change their mind and way,
And slow are we to learn that
They don't mean just what they say.

But do not be discouraged;
Just take it to the Lord;
And leave there in His keeping
Disappointments you have stored.

Then take to heart the lesson
That He alone is true;
And He alone is faithful
And really loveth you.

Just learn to trust Him only;
You will find Him always fair;
And no matter what the problem,
His loving arm is there.

1944

With Tears in My Heart—the Poems of Gertrude Grace Sanborn

God for Me

God for me?
I who have turned away
And mocked Him,
Was in times past
A stranger to His face
I who did not care--
Not even seek Him,
Nor read His word,
Nor even want His grace.

God for me?
How wonderful He said it;
My heart would doubt it
If it were not written down.
Oh, praise His name
That once He sought and found me;
And now I live
To bring to Him my crown.

January, 1945
in <u>Able To Bear It</u>

If God *be* for us, who *can be* against us?
Romans 8:31

Folio XXIV—Christian Life

He Whom Thou Lovest

"He whom Thou lovest" is sick, dear Lord,
And thou hast gone far away;
Yet thou dost know he is sick, dear Lord;
Still Thou wouldst have me to pray.

"He whom Thou lovest," is on my heart;
And upward on wings of prayer
Lift I my voice to Thy kind ear;
I know Thou art listening there.

Send forth Thy power and stay and heal;
Breathe out Thy virtue divine;
For *"He whom Thou lovest"* is sick, dear Lord;
And he is a friend of mine.

Lord, as of old in Bethany,
Thou hast a tender tear.
Faithful High Priest to God Thou art
No matter the time or year.

1946

Lord, behold, he whom thou lovest is sick.
John 11:3b

With Tears in My Heart—the Poems of Gertrude Grace Sanborn

It Is Enough to Know

It is enough to know
That God my Father
Knows all my ways
And days of coming years.

It is enough to know
He never erreth
He leadeth step by step
Past all my fears.

We do not need to know
The distant morrow
We do not need to know
Where He will lead.

It is enough to know
That God my Father
Will care for me and mine
And meet my need.

May, 1962
Set to original music by the author

Folio XXIV—Christian Life

He Goes Before Me

One step ahead I take;
He goes before me.
One day, a time, I live;
He's always there.
The years behind I see;
He keeps me trusting.
It's enough to know
I'm in His care.

MAY, 1962
The chorus of "IT IS ENOUGH TO KNOW"

And he said, Blessed *be* the LORD God
of my master Abraham,
who hath not left destitute my master
of his mercy and his truth:
I *being* in the way, the LORD led me
to the house of my master's brethren.
Genesis 24:27

A Melody in My Heart He Gives to Me

Melody of heart He gives to me.
Songs of the Lord, the Spirit sings to me.
Hymns from His Word--learning constantly,
Unfolding to me in melody.
Songs of praise--He teaches me
Making my soul sing joyously.
I sing in my heart, His melody sweet,
Those songs He gives to me.

Wonderful strains my Saviour sings to me;
Beautiful notes of peace He brings to me.
Comfort and strength His music gives to me,
So tenderly and patiently.
Deep in my heart there rings this melody;
It makes me walk triumphantly;
Keeps blessing my soul and making me whole,
These songs in my heart I sing.

Songs for each day, my Father gives to me
Staying my cares by truths' great melody
Strains from above to soothe each pain and loss
To bear the cross He gave to me.
Songs in the night, I sing subconsciously;
They stay my poor infirmity.
His poems of praise, I'll sing all my days.
These songs Jesus gives to me.

Folio XXIV—Christian Life

Psalms of His love, He brings to memory,
Giving me strength to walk courageously,
Flooding my soul with God's own harmony,
Restraining me, sustaining me;
Unto the Lord I lift my Heart in praise,
For He has led in all my ways;
I sing unto Him who causes my song,
These songs in my heart I sing.

January 1962
(Set to music)

In Days Gone By

In the days gone by
My Father guided;
In the days gone by
I felt His care.
In the days gone by
He kept and helped me;
And in days gone by
Was always there.

In the days of loss
And deepest sorrow
In the days of great
And awful pain
In the days gone by
He stood beside me;
And He helped me thru
The darkest strain.

In the days gone by
I learned to trust Him;
In the days gone by
I felt His claim.
In the days gone by
He drew me closer;
And in days ahead
He'll be the same.

June 1964 (a song)

I Forgot That He Was God

Oh, I knew Him as my friend
Who'd be true unto the end;
And I walked close by his side,
Trusting Him what'er betide.
But I forgot that He was God
And was sovereign in His way;
I forgot that He was God!

Oh, I knew that He was fair
And with grace beyond compare;
And I knew He was a King
And was ruling everything.
But I forgot that He was God
And was sovereign everyday.
I am glad that He's my God!

Refrain:
I forgot that He was God
And will have His sovereign way;
I forgot He was the Potter,
And I but earthy clay.
He has changed my life completely;
But now I know and I'm glad
That He is God!

1970 (words set to music)

With Tears in My Heart—the Poems of Gertrude Grace Sanborn

His Mercies Every Morning

His mercies are new every morning;
They fall as the dew fresh and free.
Provision and blessing sustaining,
They drop from the Father on me.

Each morning I wake and I praise Him;
I know He will care for His own.
He goeth before every footstep;
He never will leave me alone.

O wonder that He doth consider
My needs and my cares every day
And sends me new mercies each morning;
His promise supplies me alway.

O marvelous mercies from heaven;
Compassion beyond all compare;
His faithfulness great is my portion;
His mercies are my daily fare.

July, 1973

It is of the **LORD'S** mercies that we are not consumed, because his compassions fail not. *They are* new every morning: great *is* thy faithfulness.
Lamentations 3:22-24

Folio XXIV—Christian Life

O to Be Like Him

O to be like Him!
Just to be like Him!
What marvelous grace has been said
That I may be like Him,
Changed to His beauty,
The more I reckon me dead.

Colossians 3:11; 2 Corinthians 3:18
1955

But we all, with open face
beholding as in a glass
the glory of the Lord,
are changed into the same image
from glory to glory,
even as by the Spirit of the Lord.
2 Corinthians 3:18

Faith

There came a storm upon life's sea;
I hid my face in fear
I would not see.

My Lord walked upon the water ;
He bid me leave my frail craft
And step out toward Him.

I saw His eyes--
Kind, calm, and loving;
I heard His voice
So deep with care.

I left this frail craft of flesh
And stepped out by faith
To meet Him there.

1944

But without faith *it is* impossible to please *him*.
for he that cometh to God must believe that he is,
and *that* he is a rewarder of them that diligently seek him.
Hebrews 11:6

Folio XXIV—Christian Life

His Peace

Shadows lengthen on this world,
And wicked men increase;
For the child of God there comes
His grace and perfect peace.

Resting on His sovereign power
Come what may of men or fray,
He is there behind the shadows
Watching over me alway.

1984

Peace I leave with you,
my peace I give unto you:
not as the world giveth, give I unto you.
Let not your heart be troubled,
neither let it be afraid.
John 14:27

My Secret Room

I have a secret room in thought
Where I love to steal away;
Where all the things I yearn to have
Are there in good array.
The walls, a cool and shady green;
On the floor, a thick soft pad;
And windows clear
With trees outside
And birds to make me glad.
A large arm chair with tall soft back
When I am tired, to write or read,
Does make my room complete.

Within my room there's music
Which I, of course, can make
Upon my own piano
And never make mistake.
I'll write the songs and verse I hear
Which sing within my soul;
And no one dare to interfere
Or call me from my goal.

And in this room a table stands
And on it rows of books;
God's Word is first and then the ones
To make me search and look.

Folio XXIV—Christian Life

A typing writer--one which works,
And paper in all sizes;
A pencil sharpener on the wall
All this my mind surmised.
I have this secret room in thought;
I go there oft to rest.
I love each thing upon its wall;
But one thing I love best.
His very presence fills this place
And bathes my heart and mind.
What matchless peace is this to me
That I this place did find!

June 1961

Come Apart and Rest

Come apart and rest;
Just lean thyself on Him.
Do not strive; do not work;
Just rest thyself in Him.

Come away from care,
Close to His loving heart.
Do not plead; do not cry;
Just come thyself apart.

Come apart to Him;
He knows the empty place.
Look thou not to others
Just look into His face.

Come away from trying,
And let Him be thy peace.
For pented hidden sorrow,
He'll be the sure release.

May 1953

Folio XXIV—Christian Life

Looking to Jesus

Though on this journey I may meet
Great disappointment and defeat,
Tho friends may fail and turn astray,
He lovingly turns my eyes away;
Teaching me as I laugh and cry--
Cause and effect--both how and why;
Molding my life to suit His will
When to go on and when be still.

So looking to Him, His lovely face--
Light of all knowledge there in grace;
Bearing me up with arms so strong,
Telling my heart, "It won't be long";
Living and looking—O what grace!
To say a word in Jesus' place;
For He has saved me, praise His name,
And I must needs His name proclaim!

Hebrews 12:2
1944
Written for my dear Dad in an hour of trial at Grayton Road Baptist Church.

The Lord Our Banner

So tired till I found His shadow
And sat down under His calm.
So sad till I felt His compassion
On my soul as a healing balm.
So weak till I saw o'er me His banner
And knew He was strong in the fray.
So homesick to go on to meet Him;
So glad He is coming someday.

1943
As found in <u>Able To Bear It.</u>

As the apple tree among the trees of the wood,
so *is* my beloved among the sons.
I sat down under his shadow with great delight,
and his fruit *was* sweet to my taste.
He brought me to the banqueting house,
and his banner over me *was* love.
Song of Solomon 2:3-4

Folio XXIV—Christian Life

Keep on Singing the Song of Faith

Keep singing the song of faith
However dark the night.
And as you praise, the Lord will work
To change your faith to sight.

Keep living the life of trust
However dark the night.
And as you walk, the Lord will work
To change your walk to flight.

1959

The LORD *is* great in Zion;
and he *is* high above all the people.
Let them praise thy great and terrible name;
for it *is* holy.
Psalm 99:2-3

I'll Commit All My Care

I'll commit all my care unto Jesus;
I'll commit all my cares unto Him.
For I know He is mighty to save me;
So my life I'll commit unto Him.
He will take my despair and my sorrow He'll bear;
I'll commit all my care unto Him.

I'll commit all my care unto Jesus;
I can trust every burden to Him.
For he died on the tree to redeem me;
So my heart I commit unto Him.
All my grief He did share when He died for me there;
I'll commit all my care unto Him.

I'll commit all my care unto Jesus;
I'll commit every problem to Him.
For He gives me His peace and His comfort;
So my mind I'll commit unto Him.
Every doubt He will take, and He'll make an "escape";
I'll commit every care unto Him.

July 1964
This poem is set to music and has a chorus also.

Folio XXIV—Christian Life

God's Tomorrow

Take no thought for tomorrow,
For tomorrow is not thine to bear;
Take no thought for tomorrow,
No thought for its joy or its care.

The Father has given us today
To live, and to use, and to see;
And has hidden in wonderful wisdom
Tomorrow from you and me.

He knows of its pain and its anguish;
He helps us get ready to be
Equipped by the trial of the present
To walk in the new day to be.

1940, This poem is found in the author's booklet <u>Able to Bear It</u>.

📖

If then God so clothe the grass,
which is to day in the field,
and to morrow is cast into the oven;
how much more *will he clothe* you,
O ye of little faith?
Luke 12:28

Lord, Is It I?

Someone denied Him this morning
And paid to the Devil his price.
Someone betrayed for a bauble,
And someone denied Him thrice.

Someone asleep in the garden
Nor watch and pray for an hour;
Someone too sleepy for praying
To stand against Satan's power.

Someone forsook Him at Calvary
To walk up that cruel hill alone.
Someone forgot how He suffered
For all my dark sin to atone.

Someone is weeping and grieving
Tho the stone was rolled away.
Someone forgot He was Victor
That death could not now keep his prey.

Someone is sad and discouraged
Not looking for Jesus today.
Someone's forgotten He's coming
To take all His dear ones away.

Folio XXIV—Christian Life

Someone's not waiting for Heaven
Where all its glories will be.
Someone's not longing for Jesus
Waiting His dear face to see.

There at the table they asked Him,
"Lord, is it I?" they said;
There when they gathered at supper
When He gave the cup and the bread.

"Lord is it I?" they all whispered,
Fearful their own hearts to know.
For the Saviour did know who betrayed Him,
Yet on to the garden did go.
Lord is it I? Lord is it I?
Help me, myself to see
That while I am looking at others,
Thou Lord, art looking at me.

April 1962

📖

**And as they did eat, he said,
Verily I say unto you, that one of you shall betray me.
And they were exceeding sorrowful,
and began every one of them to say unto him, Lord, is it I?**
Matthew 26:21-22

Like Ruth

I've walked on life's old barren highway
In the time of the Harvest of wheat
Til I chanced to turn in by His gleaners,
And there my great Kinsman did meet.

I gleaned in the rich fields of Boaz;
I gathered His ripe golden grain.
I ate of the corn that He proffered;
And at His blest feet I have lain.

He fed me with food as I stayed there;
He quenched my poor thirst from his well.
He bid me lie down until morning;
And under His garment to dwell.

He loved me and tenderly took me,
Redeemed me from poverty bare;
And brought me to dwell in His household,
Allowed me His riches to share.

March 1968
From the author's personal study in the book or Ruth--a study of types

Folio XXIV—Christian Life

My Heart Waketh

I sleep, but my heart waketh;
I hear His dear voice in the dark.
I sleep, yet His summons awakes me
   To duties and tasks I do hark.

I sleep, but I hear His blest knocking
And His beautiful call to draw nigh.
I rise to obey my Beloved
As I wait His return from the sky.

I sleep, but my heart waketh:
it is the voice of my beloved that knocketh, saying,
Open to me, my sister, my love, my dove, my undefiled:
for my head is filled with dew,
and my locks with the drops of the night.
Song of Solomon 5:2

With Tears in My Heart—the Poems of Gertrude Grace Sanborn

God Given Memories

God gives us beautiful memories
To lighten our hours of despair
Those wonderful dear poignant pictures
That help us our losses to bear.

He gives us the power to remember
Each place and each time and detail
So that the journey we started together
May continue on memory's trail.

1952

The memory of the just *is* blessed.
Proverbs 10:7

Folio XXIV—Christian Life

My Father Loves Me

Yes, I know my Father loves me
Though I can not understand;
Yet I know his way is better,
And He holds me by His hand.

Yes, I know my Father loves me,
And He truly giveth rest;
So I take the cup He holdeth
Knowing that His plan is best.

When sometimes I feel forgotten
When my trials press me sore,
I remember that He loves me;
And my heart doth sing once more.

I recall His words of promise
That He'll never me forsake;
Yes, I know my Father loves me,
And He maketh no mistake.

When I think of how He loves me
How He guarded every turn,
And I know He does protect me
Though the training may be stern;

I will praise His name forever
That my Father up above
Is a God of tender mercy,
And He deals with me in love.

1970 (words and music)

My Hand in His

I did not think He'd let me bear
This cross while hand in His;
I walked along life's road with Him
And learned His promises.

I never thought I'd feel alone,
I walked so by His side;
Or that He'd let me grieve and weep
To desperately abide.

I surely thought He'd lead me in
Some place of service great,
And help me if on trying days
I seemed to hesitate.

I did not think He'd take me here
For hand in His I trod;
Yet tho I knew Him as my friend,
I forgot that He was God.

Yes, I had truly much to learn
Since on that wondrous day,
I put my hand within His hand
And we walked along His way.

1967

Folio XXIV—Christian Life

Only Jesus

Only Jesus, simply Jesus,
Always to His cross I cling.
In the sunshine and the shadows,
Only of His name I sing.

Only Jesus, blest Lord Jesus,
Answer to my every plea.
In the morning, in the evening,
Precious Saviour, let it be.

For my problem, in my weakness,
Only Jesus I will say.
When I'm weeping, when I'm laughing,
Precious Jesus, have Thy way.

So unworthy e'n to name Thee,
Yet I'm Thine in wondrous grace;
Falling short and oft' denying,
Keep me in Thy chosen place.

1958
*The author read this poem at the request of the pastor, her son-in-law,
on the Immanuel Baptist Church Hour, October 20, 1961.*

Sir, we would see Jesus.
John 12:21b

Contrasts

Weary,
Yet resting with a burden;
Dim eyed,
Yet clearly I can see;
Shadows,
Yet always in the sunlight;
Captive,
Yet I am truly free;
Weeping,
Yet evermore rejoicing;
Hidden,
Yet here for all to see.

2 Corinthians 4:8-9; 6:10
September 16, 1960
(set to music)

**We are troubled on every side, yet not distressed;
we are perplexed, but not in despair;
Persecuted, but not forsaken;
cast down, but not destroyed; . . .
As sorrowful, yet alway rejoicing;
as poor, yet making many rich;
as having nothing, and yet possessing all things.**
2 Corinthians 4:8-9;6:10

Folio XXIV—Christian Life

A Paradox

Life is but a paradox
As I daily walk its way;
His grace supplied
For every step
And strength for every day.

Amazing are His workings
Sustaining is His power,
For never am I lacking
On any day or hour.

Life is but a paradox
As I follow all my days.
He chastens me; yet comforts me
In many varied ways.

While often He rebukes me,
Still wondrous is His care;
And tho I may be lonely,
My Lord is always there.

Resting With a Burden

Sometime my eyes
Are dim with weeping;
Sometimes my cares seem hard to bear.
Sometimes my eyes
See Jesus only,
And all my days are passing fair.

Sometimes my heart
Is very weary;
Some days my soul can find no rest.
Sometimes I run
And not grow weary.
Some days I sing and meet the test.

Sometimes my way
Is in the shadows.
Some days my eyes are blind and dim.
Some days His light is clear before me.
Some days I know no one but Him.

Weary, yet resting with a burden;
Dim eyed, yet clearly I can see.
Shadows, yet always in His sunlight;
Captive, yet I am truly free.
Weeping, yet evermore rejoicing;
Hidden, yet here for all to see.

2 Corinthians 4:8-9; 6:10
Set to music in January 1964

Folio XXIV—Christian Life

Since I Belong to Him

Every day is a lovely day
Since I belong to Him.
He gives me power
For each long hour
Since He now reigns within.
Each morning brings new work to do
To reach some soul in sin.
So there's no time for loneliness
Since I belong to Him.

1946

Thru the Lattice

It is a stately lattice
Which is within my wall;
And there upon its workings
Grow branches large and small.
Its every vine has root and stem
With leaf and tendril, too;
And clings unto the lattice
By winding thru and thru.

The lattice stands upon His purpose
And rises straight and tall;
So great are its dimensions
I cannot see them all.
Appearing smaller on the earth
Growing wider at the top,
Yet ne'er a wind of joy or care
Can cause this frame to drop.

I rest sometimes beside its shade,
And oft it hides my sun;
At times I fear its mighty height
And from its pattern run.
Some days between its workings,
I see His purpose clear;
Sometimes I can see nothing
But leaves and vines with fear.

Folio XXIV—Christian Life

I know the gardener very well;
Yet wish to know Him better.
For He arranged my garden wall
And closed me in by fetter.
He made this lattice just for me;
He built it long ago
And placed it in my garden
To see my flowers grow.

He ne'er deserts His tending;
He bids me ever call
As He looketh thru my lattice,
And stands behind my wall.
This lattice is God's purpose--
His pattern for my life--
Composed of many workings
Thru things of care and strife.
None may disturb His method,
And none can change at all.
For God looketh thru my lattice,
And stands behind it all.

September 1961

My beloved is like a roe or a young hart: behold, he standeth behind our wall, he looketh forth at the windows, shewing himself through the lattice.
Song of Solomon 2:9

With Tears in My Heart—the Poems of Gertrude Grace Sanborn

To Know the Lord

To know the Lord
To know His Word
To know His will.

To grow in grace
To grow in faith
To grow like Him.

To show His praise
To show His way
To show His power to save.

To know His will
To grow in grace
Will show His praises today.

July 1965
words set to music by the author

That I may know him, and the power of his resurrection,
and the fellowship of his sufferings,
being made conformable unto his death;
Philippians 3:10

Folio XXIV—Christian Life

Through Jesus' Eyes

Looking through Jesus' eyes, I see
Pitiful things in humanity;
Plain to behold
The new from the old,
Looking through Jesus' eyes.

Listening through Jesus' ears, I hear
Each saddened tone, each falling tear;
No doubt at all
The need of the call,
Listening through Jesus' ears.

Speaking through Jesus' voice, I say
Beautiful words along life's way;
Each in its place,
Seasoned with sweet grace,
Speaking through Jesus' voice.

1945

**For *the LORD seeth* not as man seeth;
for man looketh on the outward appearance,
but the LORD looketh on the heart.**
1 Samuel 16:7b

Victory

Some days I'm tired and weary,
And clouds obscure His face;
But, today His Word has shown me
That there is a resting place.

Sometimes when Satan tempts me
To think I must alone
Bear my heavy burden,
I cry and fuss and moan.

I throw up my hands and murmur
Like Is-ra-el of old;
I fret and mourn and grumble
And rebel and fight and scold.

But when the Spirit speaks to me,
The storm clouds drift away;
I remember how He loves,
Falling on my knees to pray.

"O Jesus, Burden Bearer,
Please take this load from me
Or give me grace to bear it
Until Thy face I see.

So, today my heart is singing
And the world is fair to me;
For Jesus, by His Spirit,
Has given Victory.

1940

Folio XXIV—Christian Life

With All Thy Mind

Here in this world,
Perplexed and tried,
Can we keep sweet
And satisfied?
So many things do try the heart;
So many worries seem to start.
Yet, we can conquer all its kind
If we but give to God our mind.

In every way,
Thru every day
In every clime
And all the time
In every test
Thru every care
From Satan's darts and wicked snare;
Yes, we can hold to any length
If we but yield to God our strength.

'Tis His command
And it is just:
Before we serve
Love Him we must
With all our strength and mind, and heart;
Or with our Lord we have no part.
Yes, God will help us to our goal
If we but yield to Him our soul.

1962 (set to music by the author)

With Tears in My Heart—the Poems of Gertrude Grace Sanborn

What to Believe?

Un and *Inter*,
Ultra and *Hyper*,
Supra and *Neo*--
What to receive?

All of these voices
Proclaiming their dogma--
What will the poor
And simple believe?

1962

📖

Can two walk together, except they be agreed?
Amos 3:3

Folio XXIV—Christian Life

Years Ago

Years ago, quite young and eager,
Set I on this journey new;
Thought I'd grow to be a figure
As I independent grew.

Sad I found since older, wiser,
Long I've walked a woman's way;
Lost I have my eager planning,
For I walk my husband's way.

1940

📖

Wives, submit yourselves unto your own husbands, as unto the Lord.
Ephesians 5:22

The Great Psychiatrist

I have a great psychiatrist.
To Him I flee each day,
To learn the "why and wherefore"
Of things I do and say.

He has the time and patience;
His discernment is so great
As He with loving questions
Makes me my case to state.

He bids me talk it out with Him
With tears and some regret;
And then to leave within His hands
The things I should forget.

In confidence upon His couch,
I am content to lie
And open all my heart to Him
And of His wisdom buy.

This great and good Psychiatrist--
True comforter of souls--
Is my tender, loving Saviour
Who draws to higher goals.

Folio XXIV—Christian Life

He bids me by my prayer to come
In everything and say
Unto His ready ear each cause
That tries my heart that day.

For this there is no cost to me;
'Twas paid for on the Tree;
And so for counsel and sweet peace,
I go quite frequently.

February 1963

📖

**Let us therefore come boldly
unto the throne of grace,
that we may obtain mercy,
and find grace to help
in time of need.**
Hebrews 4:16 - 5:1

With Tears in My Heart—the Poems of Gertrude Grace Sanborn

Sometimes I Wonder

Sometimes I wonder
On days of strife and toil
Why all my life's a problem,
And if it is worth while.

My heart feels O so weary;
My body's tired and worn;
My cares do overwhelm me
And leave me quite forlorn.

Sometimes I falter
And nearly faint and fall;
Some days I am discouraged
And have no faith at all.

It seems that I'm forgotten,
And no one seems to care
About my heavy burden
That I alone must bear.

But then He speaks to me
And care-clouds roll away;
I hear His voice so sweet
And then I hear Him say:

Folio XXIV—Christian Life

"Just lift thine heart to praise;
Trust me; I am Thy God.
I love thee, child of mine,
I know the path you trod."

My heart's so tired and worn
My eyes so dim with tears,
I look up to His face
And past my feeble fears.

March, 1962
Also set to music.

That the trial of your faith,
being much more precious than of gold that perisheth,
though it be tried with fire,
might be found unto praise and honour and glory
at the appearing of Jesus Christ:
Whom having not seen, ye love;
in whom, though now ye see *him* not,
yet believing, ye rejoice with joy unspeakable and full of glory:
1 Peter 1:7-8

Today I Wish I Were a Child

Today I wish, I were a little child again
So I could run to mother's loving arms;
And have my tears dried by her tender fingers,
To hear His words that I be not alarmed.

But I'm no child, so I must fight my battle--
To run and hide is just a child's way--
But, O dear Lord, I need some consolation.
And is there none who will a kind word say?

I'm not afraid, but I am O so weary;
I fight my fight--it seems so all alone.
Sometimes I think I cannot struggle thru it,
And weakly I begin to weep and moan.

I turn to Thee while in my anxious thinking;
I know I am Thy little one, O Lord.
I cannot change my lot nor go and leave it;
But I can run to Thee and hear Thy Word.

March 1955
In Montreal

Folio XXIV—Christian Life

The Mysteries of Life

Sometimes I sit and ponder
On the mysteries of life--
Of visions past and future,
Of happiness and strife.

I recreate with wonder
The milestones we have passed
And hold to memory tightly
And pray the joy will last.

For we are young and moving on
And life lies stretched before us.
And small, dark clouds or deep, dead calm
May mar the blue sky o'er us.

Let clouds of life make stronger
And keep our souls alert.
We should grow wise and braver,
Not shrivel from each hurt.

When life has left us waiting
At the crossroads of old age,
Let me be keenly looking
For the turning of the page.

But here I sit and ponder
On the mysteries of life
While today my life is brimming
And is free from care or strife.

1935

Looking Back

Looking back across the years
Remembering all my grief and tears,
I tremble as I contemplate
If He had not arranged my state,
And laid this care upon my life
To weigh me down with daily strife.

Unwanted, yet it pressed me sore
While thru the press, I trusted more,
And in it all, I learned to sing
And found that prayer was everything
As I the worldly things forsook.

How oft in tears to Him I fled
And gained new strength from what He said;
In weakness I on Him did lean
And of His mind I came to glean;
In loneliness I bore my care
'Twas then, I found Him always there.

In awe I think about it all
And marvel at His loving call,
"All ye that heavy laden be
Come bring your trial and learn of me."
So looking back, I see His grace
Permitting me these years to face;
Without them I would suffer loss,
And live a life for worldly dross.

July 1960
The words are set to music with the last verse being the chorus.

He Called My Name

Into my life, Christ came one day
And drew me from my sinful way;
He called my name,
My heart did claim
That glorious day He spoke my name!

Into my life, Christ came one day
And turned my night into His day;
He called my name,
My heart did change
That blessed day he called my name!

I heard Him call amidst life's throng;
I was so weak, but He was strong.
My heart was stirred;
To Him I turned;
Amazing day He called my name!

He did not pass this sinner by,
Amazing Grace to such as I!
How can it be
He spoke to me?
O day of days, He called my name!

Into my heart, Christ came to stay,
And o'er my will He holds His sway;
He spoke my name;
I humbly came.
O bless that day He called my name!

June 1964 (words & music by the author)

No Turning Back

No turning back,
Tho paths ahead seem steeper.
No turning back,
Tho hard to tread the way.
No turning back,
For His dear voice is calling.
No turning back,
For brighter grows the day.

No turning back,
I must not halt or waiver.
No turning back,
For He has planned my way.
No turning back,
To past and distant shadow.
No turning back,
Ahead lies glorious day.

No turning back,
For faith has no deterrent.
No turning back,
To falter in defeat.
No turning back,
For when my race is over
My Lord will know
That I did not retreat.

August 1967 (Set to music)

Folio XXIV—Christian Life

Since I've Seen His Face

I have seen the face of Jesus
With His beauty fair and pure.
I have glimpsed His perfect glory,
And this world has lost its lure.
I have had a glimpse of heaven,
And its wondrous sounds I hear.
I have known His peace and promise,
And I know I need not fear.

I have read the Holy Scriptures,
And my heart is guided right.
I have read His plan and purpose,
And my soul has seen the light.
I have heard His sweet voice calling
As he clearly spoke my name
He has called me to His service.
In surrender full I came.

I'm not the same since I met Jesus.
My life has changed since I've known His grace.
The things of earth have lost their glamour
Since I have seen His lovely face.

For now we see through a glass, darkly; but then face to face: now I know in part; but then shall I know even as also I am known.
1 Corinthians 13:12

With Tears in My Heart—the Poems of Gertrude Grace Sanborn

Peace

A Wonderful peace
I have in my heart,
A precious and beautiful calm.
Though there are tears
in my heart, there is joy
And God's peace
As a healing balm.

This wonderful peace
I take into my years,
Though weary I am in the fray.
The God of all peace
Will hold on to my hand
And give peace to my heart
Day by day.

📖

And let the peace of God
rule in your hearts,
to the which also
ye are called in one body;
and be ye thankful.
Colossians 3:15

Folio XXIV—Christian Life

The Shrine of Joseph

I look outside my window
And I see upon a hill
The Shrine of Joseph made by man
To cure him of his ill.

Upon the dome I see a cross
All brilliant and aglow;
And to this man-made place they come
Because they do not know.

How dark the night to souls outside
Who do not know the way.
Christ left the cross and went to heaven
And intercedes today.

O bless the Lord and praise His Name!
I do not have to plod
Up to a Shrine upon a hill
To beg a loving God.

*The author had compassion for those who worshiped
at the Shrine of Joseph yet knew not Jesus—the only way to heaven.*

Jesus saith unto him, I am the way, the truth, and the life:
no man cometh unto the Father, but by me.
John 14:6

Folio XXV

Bitterness

Let all bitterness, and wrath,
and anger, and clamour,
and evil speaking,
be put away from you,
with all malice:
And be ye kind one to another,
tenderhearted, forgiving one another,
even as God for Christ's sake
hath forgiven you.
Ephesians 4:31-32

With Tears in My Heart—the Poems of Gertrude Grace Sanborn

The House of Bitterness

I have been to thy house;
I have seen thy face;
I have yielded myself
To thy strong embrace.

I have sat at thy table,
Eaten course by course
Of anger and wrath
Which was garnished by force.

I rose up to leave,
But I found that my hands
Were shackled to thine
With carnality's bands.

The more that I struggled,
The stronger thy clasp
Until I was forced
To groan with a gasp.

O Lord, how I need Thee!
Come take me away!
I'm weak and so helpless;
Oh, hear me, I pray!

Folio XXV--Bitterness

He spoke e'er I ceased,
"Child, this need not be;
For so long ago
I gave thee the key

To unlock every fetter
And vanquish each foe;
It's God's Holy Word,
Put away and let go!"

1944
written after a betrayal

📖

To appoint unto them that mourn in Zion,
to give unto them beauty for ashes,
the oil of joy for mourning,
the garment of praise for the spirit of heaviness;
that they might be called trees of righteousness,
the planting of the LORD,
that he might be glorified.
Isaiah 61:3

O Bitterness

O Bitterness!
Thou dost lie in wait to do thy work in Christians;
And, with great activity, spring to life
At sound of strife or strain.

Calling forth each carnal impulse--
Urging, luring, leading on
To conclude that life is vain;
Dark thou art and cruel and so unloving.

Nor forgives, forgets, art blind, tho ever hears.
Troubles all who bow before thy scepter,
Giving freely days and nights of scalding tears.
Ne'er content thou art to trouble only one heart;

But unawares will steal upon another,
And swiftly bear desires to the earth.
Wrath and anger, clamor, evil speaking
Join the fray as flesh presides and rules.

Holding court and thriving in the desert,
O Bitterness!
Self and unforgiveness are thy tools;
Binds around with incoherent thinking.

Folio XXV--Bitterness

Bears one off to dungeons of despair,
Feeds us there on memory's little morsels
With retaliation guarding everywhere.
    Oh Bitterness!

1944

*My soul is weary of my life;
I will leave my complaint upon myself;
I will speak in the bitterness of my soul.*
Job 10:1

A Bitter Lesson

I had a friend I thought was true--
He said he cared for me.
He seemed to be so faithful,
Was with me constantly.
His arm became my resting place;
His strength became mine too,
And then my heart was broken,
For he proved to be untrue.

I wept before my Father's face,
"Oh God, how can this be,
That this my friend for all these years
Has proven false to me?"
It was a bitter lesson;
But I marvel at His grace,
That He showed me human failure
So that I would seek His face.

Came awful trial and sickness
Which laid me low in pain.
I clung to Christ, my Saviour,
Who is every day the same.
He told me things in kindness--
His words, they were so true.
He whispered soft, "I love you.
And will always care for you."

Folio XXV--Bitterness

No matter how I faltered
He stayed by me each day;
He filled my heart with gladness
And never walked away.
How thankful that I found Him
And that He let me be
Forsaken and offended
So that He could succor me.

1953
for Audrey during her trials and testings when a trusted friend forsook her

Yea, mine own familiar friend,
in whom I trusted,
which did eat of my bread,
hath lifted up *his* heel against me.
Psalm 41:9

With Tears in My Heart—the Poems of Gertrude Grace Sanborn

Bitter Waters Made Sweet

I trudged along life's barren highway;
I longed for a drink from the well;
But the waters of Marah were bitter,
And no one a sweetener could tell.

Since then I have drunk of sweet waters;
My thirst has been quenched at His well;
The Waters of Life have been flowing;
My life is a channel as well.

CODA:
Bitter waters made sweet
By the Cross that He bore.
Bitter waters made sweet by the Tree.
God cast in His branch,
And I drank from the well--
It was life; it was new; It was free.

July 1973

And when they came to Marah, they could not drink of the waters of Marah, for they *were* bitter: therefore the name of it was called Marah. And the people murmured against Moses, saying, What shall we drink? And he cried unto the LORD; and the LORD shewed him a tree, *which* when he had cast into the waters, the waters were made sweet: there he made for them a statute and an ordinance, and there he proved them,

Exodus 15:23-25

Folio XXV--Bitterness

A Cruel Tongue

I'm sure that there can never be
A heart so pained in agony
As when a child loved tenderly
Has proved by words no child to be.
I'm sure that there can never be
A grief so deep in misery
As when one of the family
Has shown how cruel a tongue can be.

July 21, 1963
written in Newton Massachusetts

And the tongue *is* a fire, a world of iniquity:
so is the tongue among our members,
that it defileth the whole body,
and setteth on fire the course of nature;
and it is set on fire of hell.
For every kind of beasts,
and of birds, and of serpents,
and of things in the sea, is tamed,
and hath been tamed of mankind:
But the tongue can no man tame;
t is an unruly evil, full of deadly poison.
James 3:6-8

With Tears in My Heart—the Poems of Gertrude Grace Sanborn

Peace Today

Peace today
And peace tomorrow;
Peace in joy
And peace in sorrow;
Peace next year
Such peace as this;
A perfect peace
I could not miss.

The peace of God
He offered me
To keep my mind
From worry free.
I'll trust in Him
Explicitly
And stay my heart
Eternally.

August 1961
(set to music)

Thou wilt keep *him* in perfect peace,
***whose* mind *is* stayed *on thee,* because he trusteth in thee.**
Isaiah 26:3

Folio XXV--Bitterness

A Friend of This World?

I—a friend of this world,
How can this be?
When there on the cross
He paid such penalty?

I—a friend of this world,
Which hated my God,
When He came to this earth
And man's pathway trod?

I—a friend of this world,
Its sin and its shame
Which mocks at my Lord,
Takes vainly His Name?

I—a friend of this world,
Its evil and gloss?
Separated from it
By the Blood of His Cross?

Forbid that I glory,
Spurn the pain that He bore,
Love this present world,
And not the thorns that He wore!

Folio XXVI

Grief

**Oh that my grief were throughly weighed,
and my calamity laid in the balances together!**
Job 6:2

**Surely he hath borne our griefs,
and carried our sorrows.**
Isaiah 53:4a

What is Grief

It is an agony unexpressed.
It is sorrow, deep suppressed.
It is a gnawing within my breast--
    This is grief.

It is the pain that won't go 'way.
It is the tear that's come to stay.
It is my secret sob always--
    This is grief.

It is an aching, gripping strain.
It is a breaking at the main.
It is a silent, tearing pain--
    This is grief.

It is a babe upon my breast.
It is a child I fed and dressed.
It is a life so unprogressed--
    This is grief.

It is the room at top of stairs.
It is the bed unslept and bare.
It is the coat just hanging there--
    This is grief.

It is the sea with surging roll.
It is the tempest within my soul.
It is the storm without control--
    This is grief.

Afterward

"Afterward,"
Blessed word of peace
That keeps me hoping, trusting, waiting
Through days and days,
Through all His ways,
Till afterward--blessed afterward.

"Afterward,"
This His work of love
Which keeps me leaning, yielding, willing
Through chastening hours,
Through Satan's powers,
Till afterward--blessed afterward.

"Afterward,"
What a help to faith
Which keeps me praying, singing, praising
Through tears and strain,
Through loss and gain,
Till afterward--blessed afterward.

"Afterward,"
When in His own time
And sorrow's story
Has turned to glory;
When testing days have passed away
And peace remains,
'Tis then--"Afterward."

Mother Has Gone

My dear little mother has gone.
She has left us for realms more fair.
No longer I see her dear face
Encircled in silver white hair.

I held her frail form in my arms.
I clung to her precious worn hand.
I wish she might leave without dying,
To enter that glorious land.

No pain now, no sickness, no crying,
No eyes with their vision grown dim.
She's absent from her aged body;
And now she is present with him.

I miss her and grieve that she left us.
Her vacant chair makes my heart sad.
Tho I sorrow and weep at her going,
For her I can only be glad.

I thank Him for years that I had her.
I praise Him she trusted in Thee.
I always will reverence her memory
Till again her dear face I shall see.

Folio XXVI--Grief

This Day

This day is Thine, Lord.
I thought that it was mine
So I began to make a plan beside.
But you stepped in, and by Thy plan
Laid mine aside.

I cried at the first,
For I liked my way the best.
But as I yielded to Thy perfect way,
I felt a glow, a peace,
A calm, sweet, holy rest

This day is Thine, Lord--not mine,
And for Thy glory.
Thou has made each moment, each hour.
And since I've stepped aside, I've seen
The wondrous working of Thy power.

This *is* the day *which* the LORD hath made;
we will rejoice and be glad in it.
Psalm 118:24

Now

It's not what you did before
When you had strength and gold
But what you are doing NOW
Since you are weak and poor and old.

The Father has called us to serve Him
No matter in youth or age.
He expects us to bring a good harvest
To record on the heavenly page.

It is not if we have the talent;
It is not if we keep the pace;
But it's pressing and looking e'er onward
Till we gaze at His wonderful face!

And thou shalt love the Lord thy God
with all thy heart,
and with all thy soul,
and with all thy mind,
and with all thy strength:
this *is* the first commandment.
Mark 12:30

Folio XXVI--Grief

How Will I Know

How will I know if you miss me at church?
How will I know if you care?
How will I know that you love me
Or miss me, if I wasn't there?

A card or a note or a visit,
A word of cheer--even small--
Will help in my life's daily trial
If you would just give me a call.

How will you know that I miss you?
How will you know that I care?
How will you know that I love you
And grieve that I can not be there?

**Bear ye one another's burdens,
and so fulfil the law of Christ.**
Galatians 6:2

With Tears in My Heart—the Poems of Gertrude Grace Sanborn

As Time Moves On

As time moves on
And the past is left behind,
The things I thought I wanted
So useless now I find.

As the years pass by,
Their desires I leave behind.
Much I really longed for
So worthless now I find.

As the days come on
And I leave old days behind,
I find a brighter future
Which is better far and kind.

As the hours move by,
I care not what the way.
I find I do not want one thing
Except His peace today.

📖

But *this* one thing *I do*, forgetting those things which are behind, and reaching forth unto those things which are before,
Philippians 3:13b

Folio XXVI--Grief

Give Me This Mountain

Give me this mountain,
O Lord I pray.
Give me the victory
O'er the hard things today.

Give me this mountain;
Thy promise I claim.
Give me this high place;
Thus to praise Thy Name.

Give me this mountain;
What matter my age.
Give me provision
The battle to wage

Give me this mountain,
O Lord I pray,
Though there are giants
That stand in the way.

Grant me Thy blessing,
O Lord I long.
Give me this mountain;
I'll climb with a song.

Joshua 14:12

What Would I Do?

What would I do without Jesus?
My Light and my Life is He--
My Lord and my God and my Saviour,
My All for eternity.

What would I do in the morning
If, when I waken to pray,
He was not there to listen
Or hear what I had to say?

What would I do in the nighttime
When the hours are lonely and still?
Where could I turn in the darkness?
And who could my yearnings fill?

What would I do without Jesus
When the pain is too hard to bear?
And I weep and despair in misery
O what if He were not there?

What would I do on the morrow
When suddenly it seems I am old
And I have no strength of my own self
Only His to which I can hold?

Folio XXVI--Grief

What would I do without Jesus
When death takes my loved ones most dear?
O how could I go on without them
If He did not comfort and cheer?

What would I do at the end time?
To whom could I cling as I die?
Ah, I cannot live NOW without Jesus
And I MUST have Him there when I die.

1978

**Lo, I am with you alway,
even unto the end of the world.**
Matthew 28:20b

The More

The harder it is,
The more that I love Him.
The weaker I grow,
The more He is strong.

The more that I need Him,
The more He provideth.
Tho faintly I see Him,
The more that I long.

The greater the burden,
The more He sustaineth.
The more that I grieve,
The more that He cares.

The longer the day,
The sweeter each hour.
The sterner the test,
The more that He bears.

The more that He tries me,
The more blessed the lesson.
The more that I trust Him,
The more that I learn.

2 Corinthians 12:9

Ren & Gertrude Sanborn on November 16, 1923

What?
know ye not that your body
is the temple of the Holy Ghost *which is* in you,
which ye have of God, and ye are not your own?
For ye are bought with a price:
therefore glorify God
in your body,
and in your spirit,
which are God's.
1 Corinthians 6:19-20

Folio XXVII

Christ's First Coming

Behold, a virgin shall be with child,
and shall bring forth a son,
and they shall call his name Emmanuel,
which being interpreted is, God with us.
Matthew 1:23

Beautiful Saviour

Beautiful Saviour,
Wonderful Lord,
Amazing Mystery,
Incarnate Word!

Born of a woman
In fashion and frame,
Found as a Servant
To this earth He came.

Fulfilled the Promise,
A Davidic King
Came in "due time,"
Salvation to bring.

Down from His Glory
In Heaven above,
God sent His Son,
The Gift of His love.

Laid in a manger
And cradled in hay,
This holy Jesus,
The Truth and the Way.

Folio XXVII—Christ's First Coming

Why He Came

Why did He come,
This gracious Gift from God?
To lay His head on manger's hay
And then earth's pathway trod.

Why did He come
And die upon a Tree?
To bear the sin of all the world
And to the Saviour be.

Why did He come?
His own would not receive.
Grace it was that saved me
The hour I first believed.

Why did He come?
He came with awful cost.
Because the Father loved the world,
He was sent to save the lost.

Why did He come
And lay such glory by?
To be so poor and give his life
For such as you and I.

John 1:10-12

To Bethlehem Town

To Bethlehem town,
Ephratah the least,
Came Mary the virgin
Upon a poor beast.

Joseph protector
Beside her was he,
Guarding God's vessel,
This mother to be.

There in the manger
The Christ-Child she laid;
While by angels to shepherds
Glad tidings were made.

From David of Judah,
Yet God's unique Son;
Incarnate Lord Jesus,
The bless'd Holy One.

Incomparable Lord,
Redeemer, and Way--
O praise be to God
He was born on that day!

Micah 5:2

Folio XXVII—Christ's First Coming

Lower Than the Angels

Made lower than the angels
To suffer death He came.
My Lord came down from heaven
To bear the cross of shame.

He came into a manger,
Born of a virgin mild.
The angels told His advent,
The human holy Child.

Poor shepherds saw Him lying
Upon a woman's breast.
They bowed in adoration,
For they were purely blessed.

Wise men of East took journey
And traveled from afar.
They watched His sign in heaven,
The guiding eastern star.

O wondrous natal hour
When God sent forth His Son.
So loved the world He gave Him
To save the lost, undone.

Hebrews 2:9

O Glorious Saviour

He came into this sinful world
One holy, wondrous day;
And from the virgin's womb was born
On Bethl'em's manger hay.

He left His Father's glorious throne
In mansions of the sky;
Was born a holy, sinless Child
To live and grow and die.

Upon the cross one awful day,
God's Lamb did bear my sins away.
Three days and nights death held Him prey
Till dawn the resurrection day.

He broke the bands of sin that day
In triumph rolled the stone away.
The Lord of life death could not keep.
He rose a Victor o'er the deep.

O glorious Saviour, victorious Lord!
Eternal triumph, Incarnate Word!
He set me free, gave victory.
Now I, too, shall live His face to see.

Luke 2:11

📖

𝔉or he saith,
𝔍 have heard thee in a time accepted,
and in the day of salvation have 𝔍 succoured thee:
behold, now *is* the accepted time;
behold, now *is* the day of salvation.
2 Corinthians 6:2

**1945 Picture of Gertrude Sanborn
(Born December 6, 1904; Died June 7, 1988)**

🔔

📖

Let the words of my mouth,
and the meditation of my heart,
be acceptable in thy sight,
O LORD, my strength, and my redeemer.
Psalm 19:14

www.ingramcontent.com/pod-product-compliance
Lightning Source LLC
Chambersburg PA
CBHW060104170426
43198CB00010B/769